THE
LOVE OF GOD
AND YOU

Bernard N. Schneider
and Mary Schneider

BMH Books

P.O. Box 544
Winona Lake, IN 46590

DEDICATION

To our daughter, Lucie Marie Levy
who was a gift of God's love

Cover design by Terry Julien

ISBN: 0-88469-164-0
COPYRIGHT 1985
BMH BOOKS
WINONA LAKE, INDIANA

Printed in U.S.A.

Acknowledgements

My thanks to the many authors and poets who contributed thoughts of value to this book. A big thank you to Charles Turner who took a special interest in this book and to those who prayed that the book would be finished and a blessing to those who read it. MY GREATEST THANKS IS TO THE LORD who persuaded me through the Holy Spirit that a "labor of love" was in order and in His will.

Mary Schneider

C. H. Spurgeon, "Treasury of David" volume 2, page 86, "Luther's Table Talk."

Stephen Charnock "The Existence and Attributes of God", page 437. Poems by Arthur Vaugh and Annie Johnson Flint

Foreword

BMH Books appreciates the opportunity to bring you this fine book. The circumstances surrounding its origin and printing are a bit unusual. Dr. Bernard Schneider wrote a book about ten years ago entitled, *The Holy Spirit and You.* It was an excellent book and he received many positive comments about the section on the subject of the Love of God.

He asked permission to write a book on the subject of the importance of God's love. We at BMH Books were delighted with the prospect of such a title. When Dr. Schneider began the book he was ill, but he and his wife Mary labored at the task. He was able to outline most of the book and to write a number of the chapters. He then became too ill to continue the work and shortly thereafter, Dr. Schneider laid aside his earthly duties and went to be with the Lord.

The partially completed manuscript remained that way for some months. His wife, Mary felt the work should be completed. After some further work on her part and encouragement by BMH Books the work went forward again. This was not new for Mary since she had worked with Bernie in other writings and it became a labor of love to see the manuscript completed.

The book is now completed and we feel it will be an important work to the glory of the Lord. We feel that no person other than Mary could have completed that work. She had lived with this man for years, heard him preach thousands of sermons and had shared with him in editing and typing manuscripts. She had prayed and labored with Bernie for years of public and private ministry. Together the work has been completed for the glory of the Lord.

Charles W. Turner
BMH Books
August 1985

Table of Contents

CHAPTER 1

The Love of God,
The Keynote of the Bible

Suggested reading: I Cor. 13, John 13:1-16, Luke 15:11-32

What is love? Webster says, "A strong affection or liking for someone or something." In describing a lover, Webster tells us, "One who greatly enjoys something." When we are in love we *feel* love and *display* love by our actions. In our human relationships love seems to begin with an awareness that progresses into a state of strong attraction. From strong attraction love changes to tender feelings, a compassionate attitude, a solicitude, a protective attitude and becomes a tie that is not easily broken. Love makes us flexible. We have to be flexible to understand and adjust to the attitudes and actions of others that we love. Love also engenders patience and supplies strength for the impossible task. It is love that gives us the willingness to sacrifice in order to give happiness.

When we come to the love of God, it is difficult for us to understand the greatness, goodness and fullness of His love in our lives. We are constantly influenced with what the world thinks is love as it comes our way via television, magazines, and sometimes an off-color joke. Someone once said, "The word 'love' needs a bath," meaning, of course, this sort of love. But we find God's love uncorrupted and unspoiled. *His* love is truly the keynote of the Bible, permeating every book.

The greatest sentence ever written is made up of just three words, GOD IS LOVE. I John 4:8.

In I Cor. 13 Paul gives us these characteristics of love.

Patience: Love understands and therefore waits.

Kindness: Love in action.

Generosity: Love envieth not.

Humility: Love vaunteth not itself, is not puffed up.

Courtesy: Doth not behave itself unseemly.

Unselfishness: Seeketh not her own.

Good temper: Is not easily provoked.

Guilelessness: Thinketh no evil.

Sincerity: Rejoiceth not in iniquity, but rejoiceth in the truth. In the concluding verse of this chapter, Paul states, "And now abideth faith, hope, love, these three; but the greatest of these is love." Notice, faith is great, hope is great, but *the greatest of these is love.*

In I John 4:7-10 we are told several things about love.

First: We are to love one another for love is of God. In I Peter 1:22 we read ". . . see that ye love one another with a pure heart fervently."

Second: If we don't love, we do not know God for God is love.

Third: God gave proof of His love by sending His only begotten Son into the world that we might live through Him. "For God so loved the world that He gave His only begotten Son that whosoever believeth in Him, should not perish but have everlasting life." In John 3:16 the words stand forth as a vital declaration of God's love for us. Here we find God, omniscient, omnipotent, omnipresent giving us a very clear, concise statement of His great love. He looks at the world with all its sin and disobedient people and tells us in a few unforgettable words just what He did because of love. Consider that there were many gifts He could have given — material possessions, power, lives of comfort, freedom from worry. But it was not these He gave. He gave the life of His beloved Son. His Son, His greatest gift, He gave freely *for a purpose.* He knew of the ultimate outcome of human life and to the believer He declares "You shall not perish."

Surely, trials come to the believer (James 1:2 and I Peter 1:7). He will be tempted, fail the Lord, suffer loss and illness but in the end he will *not perish* because of His faith in God's Son as His Saviour and Lord. God has promised eternal life. And in this one small verse God wraps up His good news and implants it in our hearts. These words, from the heart of God were given to all the world and demonstrate that God is as He claims, love. The Bible states in I John 4:10, "Herein is love, not that we loved God, but that He loved us, and sent His Son to be the propitiation (covering) for our sins."

Strictly speaking, God's love is not just one of His attributes but is His very own nature. As we study the Word of God we discover that love is the main motive within God for all that He does. He is love and His whole creation was formed to provide an outlet for His love. And what is the principal object of that love? The answer is man, who was created in His own image. Man is and always has been the center and focal point of all God's love.

God's Love Is Everlasting and Eternal

The prophet Jeremiah speaking to Israel said, "The Lord hath appeared of old, saying, yea, I have loved thee with an everlasting love: therefore, with loving-kindness have I drawn thee." Jeremiah 31:3. From Isaiah 54:8 "But with everlasting kindness will I have mercy on thee, saith the Lord, thy Redeemer."

We repeat: God's great gift through His Son is *eternal* life. Romans 6:23 tells us "For the wages of sin is death, but the gift of God is eternal life through Jesus Christ, our Lord."

The things with which we surround ourselves are not eternal or everlasting. We put a lot of our time and money into homes, cars, clothes and appliances. These things wear out and even we wear out. Marital love does not last. The divorce rate grows every year. Married couples seem to need a counselor or some sort of heavenly glue to keep going and be happy. In contrast, God's love lasts! It doesn't wear out or change, it can't be stolen and it never deteriorates.

Like God Himself, His love is without beginning and without end. It never was started and never will stop. Before the foundations of the earth were laid, God loved us. II Tim. 2:19 "Nevertheless the foundation of God standeth sure, having this seal, The Lord knoweth them that are his: . . ."

God's Love Is Universal,
Including All Members of the Human Family

No one is excluded from that love. God loves regardless of color or race, circumstances or location. As we travel we find many kinds of prejudice. Each country seems to have its own peculiar set. Prejudice is one of the most difficult of all sins to eradicate from the human heart. If we are steeped in prejudice from babyhood it takes the Holy Spirit to make us see that God loves every single person.

One of our good friends told us that when he went to Moody to study he was shocked to find himself singing in the choir with black people. He remarked, "It took the Holy Spirit to make me see things differently." In our first pastorate we had a dear Christian woman who was blessed with insight into the Word of God. One day she asked, "Brother Schneider, do you really think colored people have souls?" In this one point she was woefully ignorant.

We can repeat John 3:16 and still have doubts that God loves everyone on our planet just as He does us. Could God have loved Hitler? Does He love murderers and sadists? God's love does not exclude anyone. Human behavior produces great sin. God does not love any type of sin, he hates it, but He still loves the sinner.

God's Love Is Sacrificial

Romans 5:8 "But God commendeth his love toward us in that, while we were yet sinners, Christ died for us." The word "commendeth" in the Greek means "demonstrates." The death of Jesus Christ, God's Son, demonstrates to us God's amazing love for us all. In the death of His Son, we can see the depth of love God has for us. That love is so great that only the little adverb "so" could describe it. When we are faced with calvary we find a heavenly measurement of God's sacrificial love.

"He who spared not His own Son, how shall He not freely give us all things." Rom. 8:31-32. And in I John 3:16 we read, "Hereby perceive we the love of God, because he laid down his life for us; and we ought to lay down our lives for the brethren."

The story is told of a man named Cyrus who had to deal with a great chieftain called Cagular who tore to shreds and completely defeated various detachments of Cyrus' army who were sent to subdue him. Finally the emperor, Cyrus gathered his whole army, surrounded Cagular, captured him, and brought him to the capital for trial and execution. On the day of the trial he and his family were brought before Cyrus — Cagular, a fine looking man of more than six feet, with clear complexion and fearless blue eyes; his wife, a noble woman, the worthy mate of such a man; and two children, with golden ringlets hanging around their bright, childish faces. So impressed was Cyrus with the appearance of the four that he said to Cagular: "What would you do should I spare your life?"

"Your majesty, if you spared my life I would return to my home and remain your obedient servant as long as I live."

Again Cyrus asked a question, "What would you do if I spared the lives of your children?"

"Your majesty, if you spared the lives of my children I would gather my scattered forces, place your banner above them, and lead them to victory on every field."

"What would you do if I spared the life of your wife?"

"Your majesty, if you spared the life of my wife, I would die for you."

So moved was the emperor that he freed them all and returned Cagular to his province to act as governor.

Upon arriving at their little home, Cagular gathered his little family around the fireside which they had never expected to see again.

"Did you notice," he said to his wife, "the marble at the entrance of the palace of the emperor — the different colors matching with one another and the figures so perfectly formed?"

"I did not notice the marble at the entrance of the palace," she replied.

"Did you notice the tapestry on the wall as we went down the corridor into the throne room? The figures were as natural as if alive, and the colors blended as the rays of the evening sunset."

"I did not notice the tapestry on the wall in the corridor leading to the throne room."

"Surely you noticed the chair on which the emperor sat. It seemed that it must have been carved from one lump of pure gold, and with such skill of craftsmanship as I've never seen before."

"I did not notice the golden chair on which the emperor sat."

"Well," said Cagular in surprise, "what did you see as we stood before the emperor?"

"I beheld only the face of the man who said he would die for me!"

God's Love Is Unselfish

The act of sending his son into the world demonstrates to us forever that God's love is unselfish. He has knowledge of our need of deliverance from sin and with unselfish love gave His son to provide for that need. In contrast to human love, which is often selfish, we find God's love has none of this element. The love of God has for its objective this question, "What is best for the one who is loved?"

A verse which shows the unselfish love of God is found in I John 4:10, "Herein is love, not that we loved God, but that He loved us, and sent his son to be the propitiation for our sins." God has no need for Himself except to find someone to love. God is forever giving and providing for others. It is true that He longs for the response of love from those whom He loves. But His love does not depend on our loving Him, for God is love. His great objective is the happiness of His creatures.

The Bible tells us many facts about the love of God. For instance:

Love is as strong as death.	Song of Solomon 8:6
Love is everlasting.	Jer. 31:3
Love works for good.	Rom. 13:10

Love works no ill.	Rom. 13:10
Love fulfills the law.	I Tim. 1:5
Love covers sins.	I Peter 4:8
Love is of God.	I John 4:7
Love is God.	I John 4:8
Love grows roots.	Eph. 3:17
Love seeks the lost.	Luke 15:4
Love is not burdensome.	I John 5:3
Love destroys fear.	I John 4:18
Love is a commandment:	
to love one another	John 15:12, 17
to love God	Deut. 6:5
Love is fervent.	I Peter 4:8
Love is a part of Grace.	I Tim. 1:14
Love is generous.	Psalm 37:4
Love is practical.	Luke 10:33
Love is a force.	II Cor. 5:14,15
Love is a banner.	Song of Solomon 2:24

A quick glance through the Bible reveals that God is said to love the following:

a. He loved His Son Jesus Christ.
See Matt. 3:17 "And lo, a voice from heaven, saying, This is my beloved Son, in whom I am well pleased." Also John 15:9.

b. God loves His own children by faith.
John 16:27 "For the Father Himself loveth you, because you have loved me, and have believed that I came from God." Also see John 15:9.

c. God loves the children of Israel.
Romans 11:28 "As concerning the gospel, they are enemies for your sakes; but as touching the election, they are beloved for the fathers sakes." Also see Isaiah 43:4 and Hosea 11:1, 8, 9.

d. God loves the unsaved people of the world.
Romans 5:8. "But God commendeth his love toward us in that while we were yet sinners, Christ died for us." And Eph. 2:4, 5, But God who is rich in mercy, for his great love with which He loved us, even when we were dead in sins, hath made us alive together with Christ (by Grace ye are saved). Also see Titus 3:4 and John 3:16.

It may be true that the love of God toward these four groups of people is a different kind of love in each instance. The fact remains, however, that all men are loved by Him, for man is made in God's own image.

God's Love Is Undeserved

God's love is not the result of man first loving God, or by anything else within or about man. A person usually loves another person because he or she was first loved by that person or because there is something in that person that is attractive. In other words, our love is usually caused by something the person we love either does or is. It is not this way with God's love. He just loves us.

In John 4:10 we read: "not that we loved God, but that He loved us." Here we have an important principle of love that will help us in our relationship with other people. To be loved, we must love first, just as God loved us first.

Consider Deuteronomy 7:7, 8. "The Lord did not set His love upon you nor choose you, because ye were more in number than any people; for ye were the fewest of all people, but because the Lord loved you, and because he would keep the oath which he had sworn unto your fathers . . ."

These verses, spoken to Israel reveal the fact that there was nothing in mankind that God should love us. He found nothing attractive in us. We were actually worthless. Nor did He love us so that we would love Him back. It is true that He wants us to love Him, but He loves us anyhow for "God is love." The sooner we understand this great truth, the better we will serve Him in love.

As a pastor I asked those who responded to the invitation to accept Jesus Christ as their saviour, to meet with me in the study. My goal was to answer any questions and to encourage a new child of God to begin a new life since he or she was a new creature in Christ. I always said, "God loves you, never forget this truth. If you fail and fall He loves you with a love that is sad. When you are walking with God and in His will he loves you with a love that is glad. But whichever way it may be, He keeps right on loving you."

One thing we know: No human being thought of or sought God first. God thought of us in love long before we were born. Later on, in His love He sent the Holy Spirit to bring conviction of sin and an invitation to surrender to God who is love. Romans 5:8.

Let us read the Scripture which tells of the last supper in the upper room (John 13:1-16). It is well for us to remember that our Lord knew that within a few hours Peter would deny him and all the rest would forsake him. Yet, Jesus kept right on loving all of them, including Peter and including Judas, His betrayer. He kneeled before Peter and Judas and washed their feet. God's love is not like ours which is sometimes weak and sometimes strong. His love is unchangeable, constant, the very essence of Himself.

God's Love Never Fails

"Love never faileth." I Cor. 13:8. Other wonderful verses are found in Romans 8:38, 39. "Nor any other creature shall be able to separate us from the love of God which is in Christ Jesus our Lord." Or think of the meaning of John 13:1 "Having loved His own that were in the world He loved them unto the end."

The death of Christ is the greatest proof of God's unfailing love. Jesus rightly said, "Greater love hath no man, than a man lay down his life for his friend." (John 15:13). But God's unfailing love is even greater than this, for "God commendeth His love toward us in that while we were yet sinners Christ died for us" (Rom. 5:8).

At this point I think of a great evangelist, Dwight L. Moody. He contrasted a discovery of God's love as being somewhat like Columbus discovering America.

When Columbus landed he was no doubt thrilled and enchanted. It was a great event in history. But as Columbus stood on the shore thanking God, he saw only a very small part of his discovery. He couldn't see the mountains, the valleys, the broad plains or the great lakes. It is much like this as we delve into Scripture which concerns the love of God for His children. We can only realize a portion of what is involved. There will be surprises when we reach heaven and we understand more fully.

A simple but true definition says that love is the warm acceptance of another person as he or she is. Notice the word "warm". Love does not chill our communion with God or our fellowmen. Love removes any barrier and seeks fellowship. Important to remember is that love accepts an individual as he is. This is sometimes difficult to do. Through love this comes to pass. God has no such problem in having a love-relationship with His children. This is because He is love, eternal and constant. Romans 3:38, 39. "For I am persuaded that neither death, nor life, nor angels, not principalities, nor power, nor things present, nor things to come, nor height, nor depth, nor any other creature shall be able to separate us from the love of God, which is in Christ Jesus, our Lord.

We Are Urged To Love One Another

Evidently Peter saw a lack of love in the Christian of his day. Perhaps their love was not constant and sacrificial, not especially kind, long suffering; perhaps their love showed envy or pride and was not the kind of love that bears, believes, hopes, and endures all things. This is the standard of God's love and it is His desire that it should flow outward from us to others, even to those who do not agree with us or disappoint us. In love, there is some sacrifice involved. Those of "Like precious faith" are precious, not only to the Lord but to us. See I Peter 1:22 ". . . love one another with a pure heart fervently." Also see I John 4:11. This truth needs to grip our hearts. How can we who are the recipients of God's great and gracious love treat others with selfishness, spite, malice, or cold indifference?

The Best Way To Love God Back

The best way to love God back is by obedience. "For this is the love of God, that we keep His commandments, and His commandments are not grievous." The apostle John recorded the words of Jesus, "If any man love me, he will keep my word." John 14:23. In other words, obedience is the proof of our love for God. This is not the obedience of fear because the love of God takes away all fear of Him. This is stressed by John, "There is not fear in love; but perfect love casteth out fear: because fear hath torment. He that feareth is not made perfect in love." (I John 4:18).

When we begin to understand God's love we find a peace and joy in our Christian walk that we never experienced before. This love, so different from romantic love, appears about 150 times in the New Testament. Percy Bysshe Shelly, the poet, called love "the universal thirst for a communion not merely of the senses, but of our whole nature." John Wesley said, "All learning without love is splendid ignorance." A more modern writer said, "It is possible to give without loving, but it is not possible to love without giving" — Angel Martinez.

"O love that wilt not let me go,
I rest my weary soul in Thee;
I give Thee back the life I owe,
That in Thine ocean depths its flow
May richer, fuller be."

CHAPTER 2

The Love of God As Seen In Sending His Son Into the World

We have seen in Chapter One that God demonstrated for all time His love toward us by sending His Son, whom He loved, into the world to be the covering for our sins. As someone said, "Our salvation is free, but it is not cheap." Our Lord Jesus Christ came to give His life as a ransom for many (Matt. 20-28). He came in obedience to His Father in order that He might through His death on Calvary save for eternity those who permit themselves to be sought and found (Luke 19:10). Without Jesus Christ there would be no salvation.

The next two chapters will concern Jesus Christ, the greatest example of God's love for us. Who was He, this Son of God who became a man? Since he is our Saviour we need to know about Him.

"When Jesus came into the coasts of Caesarea Philippi, he asked his disciples, saying, Whom do men say that I the Son of man am?" (Matt. 16:13). The answer to that question opens the door to a whole new life for to know Jesus Christ aright is life eternal. To know Jesus Christ is also the key to understanding the Bible. Knowing Him is the answer to man's doubts and the basis of true peace and joy. To know Jesus Chirst is to know what God is really like, "For in him, dwelleth all the fullness of the Godhead bodily." (Col. 2:9).

The purpose of this chapter is to set forth in an outlined form and in language that can be understood by the average person, some wonderful facts about Christ that are revealed in the Word of God. These chapters about Jesus Christ are the culmination of fifty busy years of teaching and preaching, with Christ as the main theme of every lesson and of every sermon. And after all these years, the wonder of His person is still growing in my mind and soul. I can well understand the feelings of Simon Peter who was overwhelmed by the wonder of Christ's person and exclaimed: "Depart from me; for I am a sinful man" (Luke 5:8).

It is my sincere prayer that the Holy Spirit whose special mission is to glorify Christ, will bless all who read these two chapters, creating a new desire to know Christ even better, for to know Him is to love Him.

When writers compile the biography of some great person, they usually begin with his birth, telling us where and when this person was born. Then follows the story of his life. This is not so when we tell the story of Christ. We do not begin at Bethlehem where He was born into the human family, for that was only a short interlude in His existence. In His case, we begin before the creation of our world, for He was there when the universe was created.

(1) The Pre-existence of Jesus Christ.

On July 5, 1940, in the city of Roanoke, Virginia I became a citizen of the United States of America. However, I had already lived as a human being for 34 years, 12 of these in the United States. My birth in Germany was my beginning. Jesus Christ became a human being when He was born in Bethlehem nearly 2000 years ago, but He existed as a person in heaven throughout eternity. This is what we mean by His pre-existence. The evidence for His pre-existence is plentiful all through the Word of God. The following Scriptures are eloquent examples of this evidence.

The Old Testament promised a Messiah who would come out of Eternity. ". . . and his name shall be called Wonderful, Counsellor, *The Mighty God, the Everlasting Father . . ."* (Isa. 9:6).

"The Father of Eternity" would perhaps express in a better way the true meaning of the original words. "The everlasting Father" indicates that the Messiah, when given to the world, would possess eternity. The best explanation of what this means is likely to be found in the New Testament where we are told "Jesus Christ, the same yesterday, and today, and forever." (Heb. 13:8).

In Micah 5:2 we are told ". . . yet out of thee shall he come forth unto me that is to be ruler in Israel; whose goings forth have been from of old, *from everlasting."*

(2) Jesus Christ Himself continually claimed pre-existence.

This claim is found all through the public ministry of our Lord. Beginning in Chapter 3 of the Gospel of John, we find Jesus claiming pre-existence. He claimed pre-existence in the closing chapter.

Think through these verses:

1. "For I came down from heaven . . ." (John 6:38).
2. "I am the living bread *which came down from heaven.*" (John 6:51).
3. "What and if ye shall see the Son of man ascend up *where he was before*" (John 6:62).
4. "Jesus said unto them, Verily, verily, I say unto you, *Before Abraham was, I am.*" (John 8:58).

No wonder the Jews who heard Him make these statements were ready to stone Him. These must have seemed the words of a madman, for Abraham had lived about 2000 years before.

5. "And now, O Father, glorify thou me with thine own self with the glory which I had with thee before the world was." (John 17:5).

This is part of the prayer which Jesus prayed just before His arrest. He is simply asking the Father to restore Him to the glory which they had shared before ever the world existed. This was the glory He had laid aside when He left heaven to become a member of the human race.

The above references are only a few samples of Christ's own claims to pre-existence. There are at least 41 recorded instances where Jesus laid claim to having been sent from Heaven by the Father into this world, or where He in some other way indicated that He had existed before coming into this world, and that He remembered very well what that existence had been.

(3) The New Testament clearly states the pre-existence of Christ.

1. In the first 30 verses of the Gospel of John, the pre-existence of Christ is mentioned nine times, as found in verses 1-3, 10, 15, 18, 27, and 30. That "the Word" speaks of Christ cannot be questioned seriously, for in verse 14 we are told: "And the Word was made flesh and dwelt among us (and we beheld his glory, the glory as of the only begotten of the father) full of grace and truth." He came into the world, and that world was made by Him.

". . . Christ Jesus who, being in the form of God, thought it not robbery to be equal with God: but made himself of no reputation, and took upon Him the form of a servant, and was made in the likeness of men." (Phil. 2:5-8).

Several great and important truths are found in these verses, such as the deity of Christ, His becoming man and His substitutionary death. One fact which is plainly visible all through this tremendous scripture is the fact of His pre-existence. He "was in the form of God", before He took upon Him the form of a servant, and was made in the likeness of men."

3. The New Testament Scriptures repeatedly mention the fact that Jesus Christ is the One through whom God created all things. Carefully consider the following Scripture verses:

"In the beginning was the Word, and The Word was with God, and the Word was God. The same was in the beginning with God. All things were made by Him; and without Him was not anything made that was made." (John 1:1-3).

"God, who at sundry times and in divers manners spake in time past unto the fathers by the prophets, Hath in these last days spoken unto us by His Son, whom he hath appointed heir of all things, by whom also he made the worlds" (Hebrews 1:1, 2). Also Col. 1:16, 17 and Eph. 3:9.

Now if Christ had a definite part in the creation of the universe it naturally follows that He was a person who was active and powerful in the ages past, long before He was born in Bethlehem.

We must not lose sight of the fact that the One who gave His life to redeem us from sin is the eternal Son of God, creator of the universe. Surely, it is not unreasonable that He should expect from His own that they "Should not henceforth live unto themselves, but unto Him which died for them, and rose again." (II Cor. 5:15).

(2) The Deity of Jesus Christ.

By the deity of Jesus Christ, we mean that Christ is eternally God, equal with God the Father.

It is true that the deity of Christ is being attacked by unbelief. This is because of the Son's entrance into the human family. We believe that this doctrine is of supreme importance, for a person who believes wrongly as to the deity of Christ is going to be wrong all along the way. It is certain that God will not accept any person who willfully rejects the deity of Christ. Jesus himself insisted, "That all men should honor the Son, even as they honor the Father. He that honoreth not the Son, honoreth not the Father which hath sent Him (I John 5:23).

Because of the supreme importance of this doctrine, we shall carefully present the clear and conclusive evidence of the Scriptures, so that all doubt may be removed from the reader's mind and he will be completely convinced that the Saviour who died to save us is indeed Very God of Very God.

(1) We believe Jesus Christ is God because the Old Testament Scriptures promised the coming of a Saviour who would be God.

"His name shall be called . . . the Mighty God" (Isa. 9:6).

The Hebrew words, translated "The Mighty God" are "El Gibbor". El means God and Gibbor means the mighty one. In the very next chapter of Isaiah the same words appear and again are translated "the Mighty God". (See Isaiah 10:21).

Look at the usage of the same words in Jeremiah 32:18 where we read: "The great, the Mighty God, the Lord of Hosts is his name." Here is the same name used of God Almighty as that which was to be given to the "child to be Christ." The Messiah promised in the Old Testament is El Gibbor, the Mighty God.

Behold, a virgin shall conceive, and bear a son, and shall call his name Immanuel" (Isa. 7:14).

Immanuel means "God with us", as interpreted for us in the New Testament (see Matt. 1:23).

". . . And this is the name whereby he shall be called: THE LORD OUR RIGHTEOUSNESS" (Jer. 23:6).

(2) We believe Jesus Christ is God because He is called God repeatedly in the New Testament Scriptures. For example, "The Word was God . . . and the Word was made flesh and dwelt among us (John 1:1 with verse 14).

". . . The church of God, which he hath purchased with his own blood" (Acts 20:28).

". . . whose are the fathers, and of whom, as concerning the flesh, Christ came, who is over all, God blessed forever, Amen" (Rom. 9:5).

"Let this mind be in you, which was also in Christ Jesus; who being in the form of God, thought it not robbery to be equal with God" (Phil. 2:5-6).

"For in him (in Christ) dwelleth all the fullness of the Godhead bodily" (Col. 2:9).

"And without controversy great is the mystery of godliness, God was manifest in the flesh . . ." (I Tim. 3:16).

"Looking for that blessed hope, and the glorious appearing of the great God and our Saviour Jesus Christ" (Titus 2:13).

"And we know that the Son of God is come, and hath given us an understanding, that we may know him that is true, and we are in him that is true, even in *His Son Jesus Christ. This is the true God* and eternal life." (I John 5:20).

Why are we introducing so many Bible verses? Because we are living in an age of uncertainty and scepticism. It is a great relief to turn to the Word of God and find assurance. We need the blessed assurance of Scripture to have confidence and peace. Jesus Christ, our Lord, never spoke in the conjunctive mood when he taught the truth; there were no "ifs" or "maybes" but always "verily, verily . . .". And especially do we need the assurance of Scripture when we witness. Imagine hiring a guide who would tell you "I hope I know the way." You would find another guide very quickly. The Christian who has no assurance in the Word of God will lack the confidence needed to be an effective witness.

(3) We believe that Jesus Christ is God, because He claimed to be God.

We must remember that Jesus made this claim to many people. Sometimes they were hostile. But Jesus never "backed down" in any of the circumstances. Sometimes those around Him wanted to worship Him. He received worship as His right. He was God and He maintained that claim through His entire ministry.

Listed are six verses which tell us just what He claimed.

1. He claimed equal authority and power with God the Father. *"For as the Father* raised up the dead and quickeneth them, even so the Son quickeneth whom he will" (John 5:21).

2. He demanded equal authority and power with God the Father. "That all men should *honor the Son, even as they honor the Father"* (John 5:23).

3. Christ claimed to be One with the Father. *"I and the Father are one"* (John 10:30).

The next few verses tell us that the Jews tried to stone Him because "that thou, being a man, makest thyself God." See John 14:9.

4. Jesus claimed to forgive sin, which only God can do. "When Jesus saw their faith, he said unto the sick of the palsy, "Son, thy sins be forgiven thee" (Mark 2:5). The rest of the story of the healing of the sick man is additional proof of His deity that is offered to the Jews by displaying His supernatural power.

5. Christ promised to give eternal life to those who received Him. "And I give unto them eternal life . . ." (John 10:28).

6. Jesus Christ received worship and encouraged it. Yet, worship belongs only to God according to Christ Himself (See Luke 4:8). In all eight instances are recorded in the Gospels where Jesus received worship without protest. For examples, compare Matt. 28:9, 10 and John 9:35-38.

It is interesting to compare Christ's attitude with that of Paul's, who recoiled with horror when people tried to worship him. (Acts 14:11-15).

(4) We believe that Jesus Christ is God because He insisted that the attitude toward Him must be the same as the attitude toward God.

When we consider the following Scriptures with an open mind there is only one conclusion we can come to, and that is that the *Christ of the Bible is God.* In Christ, God came to earth to be seen and heard, When we see Christ at work, we see God at work. When we behold Christ's attitude toward those in need, those in sorrow, those caught in sin, those steeped in self-righteousness, we behold there the attitude of God toward people. If Christ is not God, we would have to rewrite the Bible.

1. Jesus Christ declared that to honor Him was to honor God and to not honor Him would be the same as refusing to honor God. "That all men should honor the Son, even as they honor the Father. He that honoreth not the Son, honoreth not the Father which hath sent Him" (John 5:23).

2. Jesus asserted that to see *Him* was to see God. "He that hath seen me, hath seen the Father " (John 14:9).

And "he that seeth me seeth him that sent me." (John 12:45).

3. Christ implied that to believe in Him was to believe in God, and to refuse to believe in Him was to refuse to believe in God. "He that believeth in God, believeth not on me but on Him that sent me" (John 14:44). And — "ye believe in God, believe also in me" (John 14:1).

4. Jesus even insisted that to hate Him was to hate God. "He that hateth me hateth my Father also." (John 15:23). These words are as plain and as strong as words can be, leaving no doubt whatever that Jesus insisted that whatever treatment people bestowed upon Him is also accorded to God.

When we hear Jesus say, "Behold, I stand at the door and knock" we should understand that it is God knocking at our door, and to refuse Him entrance is to refuse God. "For in Him dwelleth all the fullness of the Godhead bodily."

It is a fact that mankind has a strong desire to see that which he worships. Consider the image of Buddha which is gross and ugly. Think of the African idols of heathen religion. The only reason a sane person would bow in worship before something so ugly is that he wants to see his God. Visual contact brings him closer and gives more purpose to worship.

Job lamented that although he sought for God, He could not see Him. ". . . I cannot behold Him" (Job 23:8, 9).

Phillip had this longing when he said, "Lord show us the Father and it sufficeth us" John 14:8.

When we were in Venice, Italy, I followed a stream of people into a church. I was just curious at what might be happening there.

Behind a railing stood a priest and in his hands he held an object which looked something like an urn. People knelt before the railing and I was surprised to see tears coursing down their cheeks. My thoughts were like this: "Oh, you dear people, if you could only see Jesus! Your adoration would not be wasted. Is there anything in that urn that you can truly worship? Don't you know about the One who loved you and died for you? There is One that we can see very clearly in the four Gospels. It is God's own Son, Jesus Christ who "forsook the courts of everlasting day, and chose with us a darksome house of clay." (Milton)

(5) We see the love of God in the incarnation of Jesus Christ. By the Incarnation of Jesus Christ we mean that supernatural act whereby the Second Person of the Godhead became a human being with a human nature, human flesh, and a human form. The word INCARNATION literally means THE COMING INTO FLESH.

When Jesus was born in Bethlehem, physically He was born just like any other baby. There was a big difference in the child Himself who was the sinless Son of God. This had never happened before. He was begotten by the Holy Spirit, even though He was born of a human mother. His birth was foreshadowed in the early chapters of Genesis "And I will put enmity between thee and the woman, and between thy seed and *her seed*; it shall bruise thy head, and thou shalt bruise his heel." (Gen. 3:15).

The following 12 verses tell us more about His birth:

1. "Being in the form of God . . . (he) took upon himself the form of a servant, and was made in the likeness of men" (Phil 2:6-7).

2. "God sent forth his Son, made of a woman . . ." (Gal. 4:4).

3. ". . . Jesus, who was made a little lower than the angels" (Heb. 2:9).

4. "Took part of flesh and blood" (Heb. 2:14).

5. "When he cometh into the world, saith . . . a body hast thou prepared me" (Heb. 10:5).

6. "God sending his own Son in the likeness of sinful flesh" (Rom. 8:3).

7. "Made of the seed of David according to the flesh" (Rom. 1:3).

8. "The Word was made flesh" (John 1:14).

9. "He became poor" (2 Cor. 8:9).

10. "God was manifested in the flesh" (1 Tim. 3:16).

11. Christ is "The second man, the Lord from heaven" (1 Cor. 15:47).

12. "Christ Jesus came into the world" (1 Tim. 1:15).

The Bible clearly teaches that Christ became a human being by being born of a human mother, a virgin, without a human father, through the miraculous action of God.

God *chose* that the Saviour would come into the world in this manner. Was He not the God of creation? Had He not created a whole world and Adam and Eve? The virgin birth of Jesus is present in God's promises of a coming Saviour. In the Old Testament we find Isaiah stating, "Therefore the Lord himself shall give you a sign; Behold a virgin shall conceive, and bear a son, and shall call his name Immanuel." (Isa. 7:14).

The correct translation of Gen. 3:15 would read: "He (the woman's seed) shall bruise thy head." This is certainly very significant, that in the first mention of the coming Saviour, He is said to be the woman's seed, and not the man's seed.

The Virgin Birth of Christ was necessary in order that *He would have a sinless nature.* We find Luke referring to this in Luke 13:5. "Therefore also that the holy thing which shall be born of thee shall be called the Son of God."

If Jesus Christ had not been born sinless, He would have been dominated by sinful nature. He could not have been a Saviour from sin. He would have been an ordinary person who would not be able to deliver us from sin and perhaps the best that He could offer would be to keep the Law. He might have become a martyr with high principles as some people believe. His death on the cross would have indeed been a foolish mistake. There would have been no power of God behind His death and resurrection. There would be no forgiveness of our sin, for only God can forgive sin. The New Testament would be cluttered with wrong statements, losing all authority.

(6) The Divine Purpose of the Incarnation.

Some critics of the sinlessness of Jesus Christ tell us that as Mary had a sinful nature, so Jesus had a sinful nature because He was her child. In Luke 1:35 . . . "The Holy Spirit shall come upon thee, and the power of the Highest shall overshadow thee; therefore also that holy thing which shall be born of thee shall be called the Son of God." This was followed by the statement that "with God nothing shall be impossible." (verse 37). We know this is a miracle but our God is a God of miracles.

CHAPTER 3

The Love of God As Seen
In the Humanity of His Son

Jesus Christ who walked the earth and lived among us for thirty-three years was and is God. But this same Jesus was also a man, fully human like any other human being, except that He was sinless. In Him Godhood and manhood, deity and humanity, were perfectly blended and He was "full of grace and truth".

Wherever we follow Christ in His earthly life and ministry, we see His two-fold nature, that of being both God and man.

As man He would get weary and He had to stop and rest. As God He said "Come unto me all ye that labor and are heavy laden, and I will give you rest."

As a man He would get hungry. As God He fed thousands of hungry people with one small lunch.

As a man He fell asleep in spite of a storm that tossed the boat in which He slept. As God He rose up and commanded the tempest to hush, and it hushed.

As a man He wept at the grave of His friend, Lazarus. As God He called, "Lazarus, come forth," and Lazarus stepped out of the tomb.

Sometimes we wonder which is more important, Christ's deity or His humanity, but we need not wonder for both are equally important to our salvation. To the Believer, the fact that Christ is perfectly human is of special significance and when truly understood, brings great confidence and blessing. In this brief study of the humanity of Christ we will consider the evidence of His being fully and truly human.

Jesus Christ Was Born
of a Human Mother

Galatians 4:4 makes this clear. "But when the fulness of the time was come, God sent forth his Son, made of a woman, made under the law."

We should also carefully read Luke 2:4-7.

We should understand that the life and ministry of Jesus Christ was under the control of the Holy Spirit. As God, before His pre-existence, He had no need for the Holy Spirit. As a man, with a true human nature, He was in constant need of the Holy Spirit. We must never lose sight of the fact that Christ was completely God and completely man.

We can be sure that Christ was a normal baby who was wrapped in swaddling clothes like other babies and then was placed in a manger which served as a bed. After a miraculous conception it took the normal time for Him to develop in His mother's womb. He was just as helpless as other newborn babies and needed to be fed, washed, taught to walk and to talk. He was a normal human baby.

Christ Developed Normally as a Child
and as an Adolescent

Luke 2:44 tells us something of the childhood of Jesus. We know He grew and developed physically. He was strong in spirit, experiencing spiritual growth as any child grows spiritually when he is taught the Word of God. He was filled with wisdom. He gained knowledge and then learned to apply that knowledge into practical usefulness. This is the only sentence given us concerning the first twelve years of His earthly life. It furnishes nothing that would cater to human curiosity. It gives no details and reports no incidents of miracles performed by Him contrary to some stories which have been told. For instance it was told that when the children played and fashioned birds out of clay, Jesus touched His birds and they flew away, He did not wear a halo. He was just a normal boy except that He was sinless. He grew mentally, physically, spiritually and socially. Although He had supernatural powers He did not use them until He left His home in Nazareth to begin the mission for which He had taken upon Himself a human nature.

As we read of the miracle performed by Jesus at the wedding in Canaan we will notice "This *beginning* of miracles did Jesus in Cana of Galilee" (John 2:11).

The Humanity of Jesus is fully confirmed by His Human needs, Experiences and Emotions.

He experienced hunger and thirst.

"Now in the morning as he returned into the city, he hungered." Matt. 21:18.

". . . And in those days He did eat nothing: and when they were ended, he afterward hungered." Luke 4:2. Also John 19:28.

Jesus became tired and weary, even physically exhausted. "Now Jacob's well was there. Jesus therefore, being wearied with his journey, sat thus on the well, and it was about the sixth hour. John 4:6, also see Luke 23:26.

He endured temptation the same way as other human beings. In Hebrews 4:14-16 we are told "seeing then that we have a great high priest, that is passed into the heavens, Jesus the Son of God, let us hold fast our profession. For we have not a high priest which cannot be touched with the feeling of our infirmities; but was in all points tempted like as we are, yet without sin."

He suffered physical pain and physical death. "Though He were a Son, yet learned he obedience by the things which he suffered;" Hebrews 5:8.

"For even hereunto were ye called: because Christ also suffered for us, leaving us an example, that ye should follow his steps." I Peter 2:21.

Jesus displayed the natural emotions of a normal human life.

He had close friends and He loved them.

In the 11th chapter of John He performed a miracle because He loved his friends. Jesus had been in the home of Mary, Martha and Lazarus many times. They not only loved Him, He loved them. John 11:5. Lazarus had died and had been put in the grave. His sisters sent for Jesus. As He approached the grave Jesus wept. The Jews said, "Behold How He loved Him!" Please read the entire chapter, keeping in mind that Jesus had normal human emotions.

He loved His earthly family.

Jesus was the eldest of a family of at least eight. He had brothers and sisters. There is something very trying about growing up in a crowded home. The others in the family were not without sin. In John 18:26 the kinsman is mentioned who had his ear cut off by Peter. Jesus showed mercy and love for even a distant relative.

He longed for the sympathy and understanding of His friends in time of sorrow and distress. Matt. 26:38-41.

The disciples were with Jesus but did not fully understand His sorrow at this time. He asked them to watch while He went to pray. They fell asleep, and Jesus addressing Peter asked, "What could ye not watch with me one hour?" What a picture of the failure of friends! Here was Jesus in His humanity seeking the comfort of His friends. Here was Jesus, perfect in innocence and love facing many bitter hours when the malice, cruelty and hypocrisy of mankind would try to destroy Him. Satan, who was behind the scene was filled with glee. And the friends fell asleep. It was not fear of death which prompted Jesus to turn to them. It was the burden of the sin of the world which brought on His feeling of agony and sorrow. It was God bowing to God as He faced the utter humiliation of crucifixion. He could have quoted a verse from Psalms which said, "Thy rebuke hath broken my heart; I am full of heaviness; I looked for someone to have pity on me, but there was no man, neither found I any to comfort me."

Christ was moved with sympathy and compassion (even to tears) at the sight of human suffering. John 11:32-35 tells us that when He saw Mary weeping He groaned in His spirit and wept. In Mark 1:40-41 He put forth His hand and healed a leper. He was moved with compassion.

He was also moved with anger and indignation at the sight of abuse and willful unbelief. He recoiled with deep feelings when He found the temple cluttered with animals. This was His Father's house and it reflected unbelief and mocked the spirit of the heavenly Father. He overthrew the money tables and making a scourge of rope, He drove the animals out. See John 2:13-16.

He had a will of His own which was subjected completely to the will of God. It was always "Not my will, but thine, be done" (Luke 22:42).

The doctrine of the Humanity of Jesus Christ is of the utmost importance to the daily life of the believer, and its study and presentation should not be neglected. His humanity assures us that He fully understands us, by experience, and so we know that He is a kind, understanding, sympathetic Saviour and Friend. To learn more, study the second chapter of Hebrews. Indeed, we need to see Jesus!

"Is Not This the Carpenter?"

This question is the only record we have of eighteen years of our Lord's life. As with all Jewish boys He was required to learn a trade. We remember that Paul, that erudite student of Gamaliel, was also a tent maker. This carpenter had chosen His trade and we can be sure He did it well. Carpentry is a clean occupation.

In that time most of the machinery consisted of two strong hands. Carpentry is not only a clean profession, it is an exacting and artistic occupation. It is an occupation of service to others and the end result, if well done, brings personal satisfaction. The ministry of Jesus Christ lasted only three years but His life as a carpenter lasted six times as long. During that long period he worked as any other working man in order that in all things He might be "Made like unto his brethren" Heb. 2:17. If our Lord could work that long and sweat with the heat and toil, it is not beneath the dignity of any person to do honest work. He knew the strength it took, the constant vigilance to be exact, the cuts and bruises that happen. During this time He was helping support a family and no doubt, He learned a great deal about people. We can imagine that in the town of Nazareth He was a respected workman. During this time also, He was building a strong body which would be needed in His three years of ministry. It was a "waiting" time, of a humble life until God the Father would call Him forth into His ministry.

Does not this time of life have a response in our hearts? There are very few who do not work. That word "work" means that we expend out energy in some sort of task. Shouldn't we appreciate our opportunities more when we remember that Jesus also worked?

In the shop of Nazareth
pungent cedar haunts the breath.
'Tis a low Eastern room,
Windowless, touched with gloom.
Workmen's bench and simple tools
Line the walls. Chests and stools,
Yoke of ox, and shaft of plough,
Finished by the Carpenter,
Lie about the pavement now.

In the room the Craftsman stands,
Stands and reaches out His hands.

Let the shadows veil his face
If you must, and dimly trace
His workman's tunic, girt with bands
At His waist. But His HANDS—
Let the light play on them;
Marks of toil lay on them,
Paint with passion and with care
Every old scar showing there
Where a tool slipped and hurt;

Show each callous; be alert
For each deep line of toil.
Show the soil
Of the pitch; and the strength
Grip of helve gives at length.
When night comes, and I turn
From my shop where I earn
Daily bread, let me see
Those hard hands; know that He
Shared my lot, every bit; Was a man, every whit.
Could I fear such a hand
Stretched toward me? Misunderstand
Or mistrust? Doubt that He
Meets me full in sympathy?

Carpenter! hard like Thine
Is this hand — this of mine;
I reach out, gripping Thee,
Son of Man, close to me,
Close and fast, fearlessly.

— Arthur P. Vaughn

The Teaching of Jesus Christ

"Never man spake like this man." John 7:46.

The officers had been sent to arrest Jesus and bring Him to the pharisees. When they came back without Him they were asked; "Why did you not bring Him? Had He escaped? Did He resist arrest? Had they not been able to find Him?" None of these reasons were responsible for their empty hands. They had found Him without difficulty. They had listened to Him as He taught and they either forgot what they had come for, or else decided on their own that such a teacher could do no wrong.

"No man ever spake like this man" they answered. They were stating the truth, for no man ever taught like Jesus did. To consider Christ as a teacher only is a fatal mistake. But to consider His teachings as one of the evidences of His deity, will be an inspiring study.

Christ Taught With Absolute Authority. Matt. 7:24-29

"He taught them as one having authority, and not as the scribes."

As a teacher, Christ is unique, outshining all earthly teachers as the sun outshines a candle. As a rule, the greater the teacher, the more readily he will admit that his is not the last word, that there is room for further investigation and for questioning. But Jesus insisted that His word was final and that there was no other right way.

He would preface many of His statements with "Verily, verily I say unto you." For instance, when he said, "Verily, verily I say unto thee, except a man be born again, he cannot see the kingdom of God." He left no room for a difference of opinion on the subject.

When He said: "But I say unto you" He assumed absolute authority on subjects that are mysteries to man, such questions as "Is there life after death?" "Is there a bodily resurrection?" "Is there a real Heaven?" "Is there a real Hell?" "Is there a real devil?" "Are angels a reality?" He was never vague about these questions and left no doubt, speaking with certainty. Consider Matt. 5:21-28; 27-28; 43-44.

On the question of life after death He said: "I am the resurrection and the life, He that believeth in me, though he were dead, yet shall he live" John 11:25.

As to the reality of heaven, He said: "In my Father's house are many mansions, if it were not so, I would have told you." John 14:1-2.

Regarding the question of the reality of Hell, He stated: "Where the worm dieth not, and the fire is not quenched" Mark 9:44.

Is the Devil a real person or fiction? Jesus said: "I beheld Satan as lightening fall from heaven" Luke 10:18.

Concerning angels He reported: "The beggar died and was carried by the angels into Abraham's bosom" Luke 16:22. Speaking on the reliability of the Scripture, He declared, "For verily I say unto you, Till heaven and earth pass, one jot or one tittle shall in no wise pass from the law, till all be fulfilled." Matt. 5:18.

When questioned about man's chances to be right with God He asserted: "Verily, verily I say unto thee, except a man be born again, he cannot see the kingdom of God." John 3:3.

Christ Claimed that His Teaching would last Forever
Matt. 24:35: "My words shall not pass away."

It is a breathtaking fact that His words have not passed away. Though it was said of Him: "How knoweth this man letters, having never learned?" John 7:15. Christ's teachings have stood every test of time and investigation down through the ages. They have never been improved upon. They have never been proven to be in error. They have never become obsolete. They are as up to date today as when they were first uttered in Palestine. When compared with the ever changing text books of man's learning, Christ's teaching stands alone as never having to be changed. His words have passed into a thousand languages, but they have not passed away.

Christ's Teaching is Completely Free From the Superstitions of His Day. Study John 9:1-4 and Luke 13:1-5.

The world of Jesus day was full of superstitions which played no small part in what people believed and in what they did. Even the disciples of Jesus were subject to some of the superstitions held by the public in general. But not so with the Lord Jesus. Not one superstition did He endorse. When faced with one He quickly declared it to be invalid. The fact that we never endorsed a single superstition is one of the strong evidences of His divine origin. It gives meaning to his claim: "I am the truth."

Christ presented Himself as The Center of his Teaching

It is impossible to separate Jesus Christ from His message for He made Himself the center of that message. This is either another evidence of His deity, or else it is evidence of unparalleled conceit. It sometimes happens that a great mind and personality will come from a low social and economic background. Here was a carpenter who had pleased the citizens of Nazareth with His perfect workmanship, a man who had cut and measured and polished wood and now He takes the position of being a spiritual teacher. He did not look unusual. To the woman at the well He appeared to be just another Jew. After His resurrection He appeared to Mary in the garden and she mistook Him for the gardener. But as He taught He made such statements as "The Scriptures testify of Me," "I am the light of the World", "I and my Father are one", "I am the Resurrection and the life, whosoever believeth in me shall never die", "Ye believe in God, believe also in me." "For without me you can do nothing." These were strong spiritual assertions from the carpenter of Nazareth. We can believe that such teaching created a furor in the minds of His listeners. Some wanted to hear more, some would be puzzled, some would be derisive. He was a master teacher, knowing how to catch their interest. Then too, He always taught on their level using illustrations which they understood.

His mind was forever occupied with man's need of being right with God. If we may speak of Christ having an obsession, then it is His great endeavor to awaken people to their great need of being right with God.

He would try to awaken them from materialism by asking, "For what is a man profited, if he shall gain the whole world, and lose his own soul?" He used a variety of significant parables and stories such as the Rich Man and Lazarus and the Rich Fool. (Luke 16:19-30, Luke 12:16-21).

Jesus tried to awaken His listeners to spiritual need by such shocking statements as "If thine eye offend thee, pluck it out, it is better for thee to enter into the kingdom of God with one eye, than having two eyes to be cast into hell fire" Mark 9:47.

He spoke of heaven and stated that there was great gladness over one sinner who turned to God (Luke 15:3-10). He told a beautiful story of a prodigal son and pictured the God of heaven as being in a great hurry when one soul turns to Him.

Sometimes there were great crowds who came to hear, sometimes only the disciples. To the disciples He imparted precious truths, declaring that the greatest cause for rejoicing is a person's assurance that his name is included in Heaven's register (Luke 10:20), and that the kingdom of God and His righteousness is the most important matter in every person's life.

And so it was that perfect man spoke and they said, "NEVER MAN SPAKE LIKE THIS MAN!" God became man that man could become Godly.

CHAPTER 4

The Love of God
As Seen
In His Goodness

Psalm 107:8,9 "Oh, that men would praise the Lord for His goodness, and for his wonderful works to the children of men! For He satisfieth the longing soul, and filleth the hungry soul with goodness."

Five times in this one Psalm are we instructed and invited to thank and praise God for His goodness. Both the Old and New Testaments have much to say about this wonderful attribute of God. The goodness of God may be understood in a twofold way. (1) As a part of God's nature. That is, God is good, even as He is holy. As such, His goodness is the source of all that is good in the universe. (2) His goodness as it manifests itself in deeds of providing for the welfare of all His creatures.

The Meaning of the Word "Goodness" in the Bible

The basic Hebrew words are "Chesed" and "Tob" or "Tub." The word "Chesed" means to be kind, to show love. The word "Tob" means to be beautiful, to be pleasant, to be good. Together, these two words describe God as being pleasant in nature and disposed to deal in loving-kindness with His creatures. In the New Testament only the Greek word "Chrestotes" is used to describe the goodness of God. This word means primarily to be gentle, to be kind, and is even translated "easy", as in Matthew 11:30 where Jesus said, "For my yoke is easy, and my burden is light."

Generally speaking, whenever the Bible mentions the goodness of God or says that God is good it speaks of that outflowing of God's unselfish kindness and love for man, regardless of whether man deserves it or not.

God's Goodness Is Manifested In His Material Blessings

Psalm 65:9-13. The center of this description of God's goodness to man is verse 11 which reads: "Thou crownest the year with thy goodness; and thy paths drop fatness."

The Bible contains many similar descriptions of God's blessing when He in His goodness and mercy "Maketh His sun to rise upon the evil and the good, and sendeth rain on the just and on the unjust" Matthew 5:45.

It is considered to be rather old fashioned today when one believes that the crops and fruits of the earth depend upon God. However, I am fully persuaded that God controls the whole affair, from the rain and sunshine that is necessary to make a good crop, regardless of the knowledge and skill of the farmer, to the success of the operation in the hospital, for without God's blessing the greatest skill of the surgeon and the most powerful medicine is doomed to failure. This part of God's love and care is given as a witness that He is a living God and that He created the heavens, the earth, the sea and all other things. See Acts 14:17.

God understands our need of temporal blessings, even that they add joy to our lives.

He sends us:

Food and Raiment	Matthew 6:25-33
Prosperity	Deut. 30:9
Rain and Fruitfulness	Gen 27:28
All good things to enjoy	Psalm 34:10, I Tim. 6:17.

Our list of spiritual blessings is even longer.

A new heart	Ezek. 11:19
Peace	Psalm 29:11
The privilege of prayer	Matt. 7:7, 11, John 16:23, 24
Appreciation and Joy	Matt. 25:21
Rest	Matt. 11:28
The Holy Spirit	Luke 11:13
Grace	Psalm 84:11, Romans 5:17
Wisdom	James 1:5

Glory	Psalm 84:11, John 17:22
Repentance	Acts 11:18
Righteousness	Romans 5:17
Eternal Life	Romans 6:23
Faith	Eph. 2:8, Phil. 1:29
Love (fulfilling of the Law)	Romans 13:8-10, Gal. 3:24

Believing then that our material good things come from God, I am bold to say that God's blessing and goodness to us in this respect is overwhelming. He has blessed industry and the working man with work. We are all eating too much. Our homes are warm and well heated. Very few of us have to chop the wood or dig the coal to make that heat. We wear fine clothes and we ride around in nice automobiles which are equipped with radios, heaters, air conditioners. Our children have the opportunity of attending a fine school. But we still complain. What would God have to do to stop the gripes and complaints?

God's Goodness as Seen in His Providential Care

Have you ever wondered: Do events happen the way they do by chance or does God oversee and control all? Do things happen by accident and coincidence or is there a definite pattern and plan with God back of it?

There are four general theories concerning this part of our lives. First, there is the "chance" theory. This theory teaches that everything happens by chance, except as we may be able to influence the event. God is left out of all events.

Then there is fatalism. This theory holds that all is fixed beyond any possibility of change and there is nothing to be done about it. Fatalism fails entirely to give a proper place to the free will of man.

Popular with many Christians is the "partial providence" theory. As the name implies, this theory holds that God controls the big events but does not have anything to do with the smaller matters of life encountered by the individual person. This view presents the serious problem of each person making decisions as to what constitutes a happening important enough to come under divine control.

Last, we have the Biblical view of the full providence of God. Here we find that God in His providential care oversees and controls all that happens in the universe. This is what the Bible certainly teaches. The word "providence" means God's guidance of events toward the goal which He has planned. Paul gave us an excellent definition of the word in Romans 8:28 when he declares "And we know that all things work together for good to them that love God, to them who are the called according to His purpose." It is only in the full providence of God that we experience God's love and His goodness. As God has planned it we are not alone, we are not unguided and we are strengthened spiritually with a renewal every morning.

Psalm 105 is a vivid description of God's providential care in the lives of His people. The purpose of the Psalm is to praise God for His providential care. The occasion of the writing of the Psalm we find in I Chronicles, chapters 15 and 16. David had brought the ark of the covenant and set it in the middle of the tent which he had pitched for it. Sacrifices and offerings were given to God. It was a day of great rejoicing among God's people. Then David made an end of the offerings and gave to every person of Israel a gift. We are told it was a loaf of bread, a good piece of flesh and a flagon of wine. Then he wrote this beautiful Psalm to express his appreciation of God's care. As you read the first five verses of Psalm 105 check these words, "give thanks," "call upon His name," "make known," "sing," "talk," "glory" "rejoice," "seek," and "remember." These few words are a good pattern for a Christian life.

David first refers to the solemn covenant that the Lord had made with Abraham and which was later confirmed with Isaac and Jacob. This covenant was God's promise that they and their descendants would possess the land of Canaan. As we look back over the 4000 years since the covenant was first made, we can see what a hard time God had trying to preserve Israel for Palestine and Palestine for Israel!

The love of God and His providential care is shown forth all through the Bible and particularly in this Psalm. David used illustrations to show God's people the different ways in which He had cared for them. We find that God's care enfolds three wonderful elements — (1) a preventative care, (2) a permissive care, and (3) a directive care.

God's Goodness as We See It in His Preventative Care

We would like to refer to Psalm 21:3: "For thou preventest him with the blessings of goodness; thou settest a crown of pure gold on his head." Although the translation of this has been slightly changed, the thought here is that God knows beforehand our need and what we will do or would do if we had our own way. And He is there ahead of us with His love and goodness, providing for our needs and preventing us from having our own way when it will hurt us.

His providential care keeps us from many a fatal mistake. As I look back, I shudder to think what would have become of me if God had simply left me alone to do what I had in mind to do.

Is this not true in all our lives? Has not God in His goodness and loving-kindness prevented through circumstances our making utter fools of ourselves or perhaps making a complete failure of life?

I believe this truth is best understood in the light of parents and their dealings with their children. A mother's love looks ahead for her child in preventative care in many ways. She wants her child to grow up with a strong body so she sees that he or she eats a balanced diet. The baby might be a lover of sweets and can't understand why mother would be so stingy with candy. But the mother is thinking of bones and teeth, something the child cannot understand. Even if the baby has a tantrum over this, the mother "sticks to her guns" and puts a limit on cookies, candy, and sweetened soft drinks. The mother is right but to the child she might appear cruel and unfeeling.

In a real sense we are like children with God. Many of our willful notions, especially our ambitions, are childish and harmful in God's eyes. Therefore, God in His goodness looks ahead and prevents us from having our own way. Like children, we are not always filled with joy about God's preventative care.

Some people want God to let them alone. This would be a tragic mistake. We would be like a child that is abandoned in darkness. We should praise God for His preventative care. This does no violence to the free will of man. Rather, it is the care of the loving Father, who looks after us, His children, until "All things work together for good to them that love God."

Abraham was a man of faith. Hebrews 11:8 tells us this "By faith Abraham, when he was called to go out into a place which he should after receive for an inheritance, obeyed; and he went forth, not knowing whither he went." Along with being a man of faith, Abraham strayed out of God's directive will into situations fraught with temptation. He sinned against God and Sarah his wife (I Cor. 8:12) and against himself (Proverbs 8:36) by both living and telling a lie. In Genesis the twelfth chapter, God had given Abraham many wonderful promises but there came a famine in the land! Abraham decided to go south, ending up in Egypt. Sarah must have been extremely beautiful because Abraham with fear in his heart that the Egyptians would kill him and take Sarah, told her to tell a lie. She was to say she was his sister, a half-truth. It came to pass as he had feared and Sarah was taken in the house of the Pharoah. Then God intervened with His preventative care. Pharoah found out the truth and Abraham was sent away. Abraham must have been a slow learner because in chapter 20 of Genesis he repeated the same sin and deception with King Abimelech. Abraham, by his faithless action almost ruined God's plan for him. What tragedy was prevented when God intervened. And what a humbling experience for Abraham! We feel rebuked of our revengeful spirits when we think of Abimelech, a heathen king who was wronged by a child of God, was gracious and gave gifts to Abraham as well as permission to dwell in that land where he pleased. "And so Abraham prayed unto God . . ." Gen. 20:17. Our failures are often used by God to bring us back into fellowship with Him.

We will never know how many times God has stood between us and danger, both physical and spiritual. God has prevented Satan many times from gaining his vicious design on the people of God. We know this because the Holy Spirit has pulled the curtain of time and let us look behind. And it is true today that God works in the lives of His people often "preventing us with His goodness," even though we do not see His hand.

God's Goodness as We See It in His Permissive Care

God *permits* things to happen to us, even when they seem (at least to us) as entirely wrong. It is one way He has of accomplishing His goal in our lives. The story of Joseph is told in Genesis chapters 37, 39, 40, 41, 42, 43, 44, 45, 46:28-34, 47.

In these chapters we find God pulling back the curtain for us so we can see Him at work in the life of Joseph, working out everything for good, although part of the time it appeared entirely wrong. Everyone was permitted to do Joseph wrong. Yet, God was there and in control.

In Genesis 50:20 Joseph is quoted as saying to his brethren who had sold him into slavery but who now were at his mercy, "But as for you, ye thought evil against me; *but God meant it unto good,* to bring to pass this day, to save much people alive."

It is evident that God works out His wise design by permitting calamities to happen to us. At such time we wonder why God does not intervene. But that is when He is nearest to us, watching over us, knowing the end from the beginning and knowing what is best.

Joseph's first great trial came when he was first thrown into a pit and then sold to a traveling caravan of Ishmaelites who were going to Egypt. They sold him for twenty pieces of silver.

Then came the trial of Joseph's long imprisonment in Egypt. This came about because he resisted the advances of his employer's wife. In anger, she accused him falsely and he was thrown into prison. How could God permit it? In prison he was bound in iron fetters and there he spent about nine long years as an innocent prisoner.

It would be human and natural for Joseph to meditate in that Egyptian jail upon his happy boyhood. He would be remembering how the Lord sent two wonderful dreams, one in which Joseph and his brothers were in a field binding sheaves of grain. Joseph's sheaf stood upright and the sheaves of his brothers bowed down before it. In the other dream, the sun, moon and eleven stars bowed before him. Even Joseph's father, who loved him, rebuked him for these dreams. His brothers, who despised him, now hated him more intensely.

The remembrance of those dreams could have troubled Joseph greatly. After all, they had seemed significant to him. Such thoughts surely came to him: "Was I mistaken about the meaning of those dreams? Is God so limited that He could not overrule my brothers? Does it pay to live a godly life? Are the promises of God only fantasies? It was undoubtedly hard. Without his kind of faith he would have fallen into a doubting, bitter, unresponsive attitude toward God.

In Psalm 105 we read "The word of the Lord tried him." In the Hebrew the word "tried" means to refine or purify, as metal is refined by heat. Joseph was purified until everything else was gone except his simple faith. Pride was cleansed away, trusting in himself was gone and all spirit of "getting even" with his brothers was removed.

After the long prison testing, Joseph was ready for the high position and the important work that God had for him. His heart was mellow enough to forgive his brothers. His faith was strong enough to stand prosperity and authority. His love for God was appreciative enough to always give God the glory.

"He sat by a fire of seven-fold heat,
As He watched by the precious ore,
And closer He bent with a searching gaze
As He heated it more and more.
He knew He had ore that could stand the test,
And He wanted the finest gold
To mould as a crown for the King to wear,
Set with gems with a price untold.

So He laid our gold in the burning fire,
Tho' we fain would have said Him 'Nay'
And He watched the dross that we had not seen,
And it melted and passed away.
And the gold grew brighter and yet more bright,
But our eyes were so dim with tears,
We saw but the fire— not the Master's hand,
And questioned with anxious fears.
Yet our gold shone out with a richer glow,
As it mirrored a Form above,
That bent o'er the fire, tho' unseen by us,
With a look of ineffable love.
Can we think that it pleases His loving heart
To cause a moment's pain?
Ah, no! but He saw through the present cross
The bliss of eternal gain.
So He waited there with watchful eye,
With a love that is strong and sure,
And His gold did not suffer a bit more heat,
Than was needed to make it pure."

God's ways are not our ways. We should trust Him even when we feel that everything is wrong, for God is near.

God's Goodness as We See It in His Directive Care

Read carefully the story of Moses beginning with chapter two of Exodus. Consider God's hand in the whole affair! God directed from the saving of the baby Moses out of the river, through his bringing up at Pharoah's court. God even spoke to Moses from a burning bush. Moses was chosen by God to be a leader. Even Moses thought he was a poor choice. God, of course, had plans of His own. He was the one who worked through the plagues, heaping pressure upon pressure upon Pharoah until finally he yielded and allowed the captive children of Israel to leave Egypt. God directed great judgments in order to care for His people. It was significant that when He sent a thick curtain of darkness into the land for three days, the children of Israel had light in *their* dwellings. God gave opportunity after opportunity for the Egyptians to escape further tribulation. He did all this to care for His chosen people.

What should be man's response to God's goodness?

1. Man should praise the Lord for His goodness.

Again and again we read this refrain, "Oh that men would praise the Lord for His goodness and for His wonderful works to the children of men." Psalm 107:1, 2, 8, 15, 21, 22, 31, 32.

This thanksgiving must come from the heart if God is to accept it. It must be more than a routine thanks that comes from the lips. It must be more than the setting aside of a certain day or any other act which is outward only. In America we have a special Thanksgiving Day which is certainly fitting. However, in most instances this is merely an occasion for families to enjoy a holiday with no work and with a big dinner. This day should be a day of genuine thanksgiving, with the thanks coming from the heart when we have been humbled in the consciousness of God's wonderful goodness.

2. We are warned not to despise God's goodness. Romans 2:4, 5. "Or despisest thou the riches of His goodness and forbearance and long suffering; not knowing that the goodness of God leadeth thee to repentance?"

We are not to take God's goodness for granted. The word "despise" as we see it here actually means to scorn by ignoring or taking for granted.

This is one of America's greatest sins. We take the outflowing of God's love casually and act as though we deserved it. As we have mentioned before, the purpose of God's goodness is to lead us to repentance. That is, to turn from our own way to God's way. If God has been good to us we need to think about it and give Him praise for His wonderful works to each one of us.

"The Lord is good, a stronghold in the day of trouble; and He knoweth them that trust in Him" Nahum 1:7.

"Teach us, good Lord, to serve Thee as Thou deservest;
To give and not to count the cost;
To fight and not to heed the wounds;
To toil and not to seek for rest;
To labor and not to ask for any reward
Save that of knowing that we do Thy will."

St. Ignatius of Loyola 1491-1556

CHAPTER 5

The Love of God
As Seen
In His Wrath

"Therefore was the wrath of the Lord kindled against His people, insomuch that he abhorred his own inheritance" Psalm 106:40.

In this Psalm, probably written by David, we read of the children of Israel who forgot the God who had delivered them from the slavery of Egypt. Verses 21 and 22 tell us, "They forgot God, their Savior, who had done great things in Egypt, wondrous works in the land of Ham and awesome things by the Red Sea." These people, so blessed of God, began to worship idols. Without doubt, they preferred sin and Hell to God and heaven. Their sin and iniquity grew as they walked farther and farther from the God who loved them. Jehovah—God certainly had a right to become filled with wrath. If He had not been God He would have turned from them forever. Being God, when sin had brought them misery, He heard their cries and pitied them. He even caused them to be pitied by those who held them captive.

God's love is easier to accept, think about, and write about than is His wrath. We steer away from anything which causes pain or uncomfortable feelings. Then we are jolted into awareness that the Bible has much to say about God's wrath and we find that wrath is a part of His love.

In the early days of our ministry, we enjoyed the teaching of a Presbyterian minister in our city. He had become upset by the liberal attitude of other ministers in the local ministerium. He spoke from II Peter, Chapter 2, where Peter warns us against false teachers. He said, "Love is like a river. It flows through the land and causes the earth to become fruitful. But when the river loses its banks it becomes a swamp." He made us see that we must recognize the reality of God's "banks" in His love. One of these banks is His hatred of sin.

In the first place, the wrath of God is mentioned 176 times in the Bible and is the active result of God's love and justice. God has an intense hatred of sin because it brings misery to His beloved created beings. It is His fixed purpose to protect His children from sin and to destroy it wherever it is found in its many guises and disguises. Strangely, the clearest descriptions of God's wrath are found in the last book of the Bible, Revelation. We are reminded that this is in direct contrast to the so-called "Evolution of Religion" which pictures the idea of a dreadful God gradually becoming a God of love. Recent archeology explorations show us the error of this theory.

The Wrath of God Is Reasonable

When we consider sin, we would expect wrath from God. God is love and there is no effective love without wrath. There can be no safety from crime in a town or city where criminals can live without laws; and of course, laws that are not enforced help no one. If God would not punish the willful breaking of His law which David said is perfect (Psalm 19:7), there would be nothing but chaos in the universe, even as chaos would soon overtake a community where crimes would go unpunished. Sadly, the part of God's universe with which we are familiar is inhabited by mankind whose disposition is to break God's written law as well as the moral law which He placed within man. See Psalm 16:7.

If man, who himself is guilty of wrong doing, finds it necessary to make laws to snuff out the life of the worst offenders by the scaffold, the electric chair, or the gas chamber, he ought to see that God must have righteous laws and righteous punishment.

If a nation, which is imperfect in its ways, feels justified in dropping a bomb on a city and by this act destroys the lives of 100,000 people, (Most of them innocent as far as crime against any other nation) should we not grant a righteous God the right to destroy evil and rebellion when it is necessary?

Let us get this clearly in our minds: God is not a mean-minded despot who makes a lot of laws and then waits to pounce upon and punish those who break them. Man certainly finds it necessary to use drastic measures to obtain and preserve peace and order. Then, is it wrong for a perfect, sinless God to protect the universe from falling completely and eternally into evil by providing a loving, just punishment to those who willfully break His laws?

Either we have to do away with the free will of man, thus making God responsible for man's actions or else we must acknowledge that God's wrath is reasonable.

Turn in what direction one will, sin confronts us as fact in human life — an experience of the heart, a development in history, a crimson thread in literature, a problem for science, an enigma for philosophy.

In view of this, we turn with reverent interest and expectation to the teaching of Christ; sent of the Father, He came into the midst of conditions which He recognized, and with which He proceeded to deal.

In the course of His teaching, our Lord made use of seven different words when referring to sin; two of them constantly, the other five incidentally. The first of these words is poneros, which is commonly translated evil. The root idea of the word is that which is hurtful. The first essential meaning of the root from which the word comes is that of pain; and the word itself suggests pain, something hurtful or harmful. It describes the active principle which produces all calamity, material, mental and moral. This word Jesus used over forty times. With this word, he recognizes the existence of a force contrary to the good and acceptable will of God. He referred to this force, as having its fountainhead in a person, Satan.

The second word, hamartia, is the most common in the New Testament for sin. There are two suggestions regarding this word. The first is that of a failure to grasp; the second that of missing possession. It signifies failure, or the missing of a mark, as when we shoot an arrow into the air and missing the target hit the nearest tree. Jesus used this word in connection with the central purpose of His coming, that of forgiving sin. The glory of the redemption of the cross shines through the references that Christ made in His central purpose, that of forgiving sin.

What Is Sin?

Sin is any voluntary transgression of the law of God; disobedience to or violation of the divine command; moral depravity; wickedness; iniquity. Sin includes not only actions, but neglect of known duty, all evil thoughts, words, purposes, and all that is contrary to the law of God. It may consist in commission, when a known divine law is violated, or in omission when a positive divine law is violated by voluntary and willfull neglect. The seven deadly sins are said to be, pride, covetousness, lust, anger, gluttony, envy, idleness. The unpardonable sin is blasphemy against the Holy Spirit.

In Proverbs 6:16-20, we read of six things that God hates:

(1) A proud look.

(2) A lying tongue.

(3) Hands that shed innocent blood.

(4) A heart that deviseth wicked imaginations.

(5) Feet that are swift in running to mischief.

(6) A false witness that speaketh lies (A person that sows discord among brethren)

These are the evidences or results of the inner sin which is rebellion against God. These are the flowers of a crop which we ourselves have planted.

A man was being given a tour of a penitentiary. He was interested in the various skills of the prisoners. He stopped to speak with an inmate who was sewing, hesitating, he said, "Oh, I see you are sewing." The inmate never looked up as he answered, "No sir, I am reaping."

The Bible speaks of sin and iniquity. We rarely differentiate between these words because sin is sin. It is only a difference in depth. It is true that sometimes we do some lying, not from an evil intent but to protect feelings. Any deviation from the truth is lying. But consider the sin of swearing before God that this is truth, and knowing that it is all a great lie. Or consider gossip. "They say" is the introduction and something of interest is transmitted from one to the other. But when the gossip becomes malicious with an intent to harm another it becomes exceedingly sinful; it becomes iniquity.

The Bible expresses itself very plainly about sin:

Uncontrolled anger and rage	Exodus 32:19
Gossip	Proverbs 11:13
Lying	Exodus 19:11
Adultery	Leviticus 20:10
Swearing	Leviticus 19:12
Drunkenness	Deut. 21:20
Neglect of God	Exodus 18:4
Idolatry	Exodus 32:4
An arrogant, stiff-necked attitude toward God	Exodus 31:9-11
Stealing	Leviticus 19:11
Hatred	Leviticus 19:17
Trickery	Leviticus 19:11
Hypocrisy	Luke 24:51
Jealousy	Proverbs 6:24
Gluttony	Deut. 21:20
Sexual Perversion	Genesis 19:24

Lust	Ephesians 2:3
Brutality	John 19:18
Murder	Deut. 5:17
Covetousness	Deut. 5:7

And we mention rape, bigotry, war atrocities, selfishness, and self-righteousness.

The deacon of a certain church had a dream one night. He was dreaming that he had died and being on his way to heaven he was confronted with a long stairway that led upward through the clouds. An angel directed him, "As you go up the steps, write on every step a sin you have committed and finally you will reach heaven." The deacon started at the bottom and was about a fourth of the way up when he saw a man descending the stairs. He was surprised because it was his pastor. "Oh, Pastor," he called out, "Are you finished already?" The pastor gave him a hurried glance and answered, "Finished? No, deacon, I ran out of chalk and have come back for more."

There are so many sins of commission and omission. Some of us do well in one respect and fail in other ways. But we all sin. Isn't it wonderful that God loves us just as we are?

Is God's wrath reasonable? Picture a busy street and a little two year old child playing in the middle. Cars are trying to avoid hitting the child so we hear the squealing of brakes and muttered curses from the drivers. A neighbor from across the street calls the mother of the child on the phone and explains what is happening. The mother casually answers, "Yes, I know. But that is Jenny's favorite place to play. She has such a good time out there." "What a mother!" you exclaim. She puts forth no effort to get Jenny out of danger. She doesn't seem to realize that tragedy will surely come. No one would accept this mother as a loving parent.

It is one of God's attributes as our Heavenly Father to love us enough to care about our spiritual safety. He tries to keep us away from sin. It was His love for the children of Israel that caused Him to write the Ten Commandments with His own finger.

The Ten Commandments were to clarify for the people of Israel a way of purity and holiness (Exodus 19:5,6). Although we are no longer under the law, Jesus quoted from them. Paul states that they cannot impart righteousness or life (Gal. 3:21). However, he also reminds us that they serve as a looking glass for us, and that they were our school-master until Jesus came (Gal. 3:24,25).

Sin Pays Wages

What are wages? Wages are earnings. A man has a right to his wages. When we take our wages we may be courteous and say "thank you" but we do not need to do that. The wages have been earned. They are the payment in return for what has already been given in toil and effort. Wages lie within the realm of law and order and of justice and deserving.

In the first few chapters of Paul's epistle to the Romans, the apostle has much to say about sin. Paul was not ignorant of what sin is and what it does. He, himself, had lived a sinful life. His excellent education did not deter Paul from persecuting the Christians, whom he hated. He also had a ringside seat to see the atrocities, the moral degradation, the utter lack of sensitivity toward moral living in his day. He, no doubt, had seen the bodies of unwanted babies which were tossed into the streets. Certainly, he had been involved in the stoning of an innocent man. He could write and preach with surety that "The wages of sin is death, but the gift of God is eternal life through Jesus Christ our Lord" Romans 6:23.

At the first reading of this verse, the words may sound rather unpromising, for they are well worn terms like "sin", "death", "God", "gift," "eternal life." Like some of the best things in life we take them for granted because we are so familiar with them. They may suggest dry theology to some Christian people, but I assure you that when they first came up from out of the apostle's heart they were like a stream of fiery lava.

But the stream has cooled with the centuries and we might think of this verse as the same old thing. However, we must be reminded that Paul was not just a theological writer or teacher, rather he was a very earnest evangelist, forever trying to win and draw men to love and trust Jesus Christ as Saviour and Lord. Therefore, all his writings are throbbing with life and they are filled with the truths that belong to all ages and places and people.

I would like to restore the fire and passion to these words until they throb with life and cause us to face the realities of life so that we will make choices and decisions which will bring us into harmony with the will of God.

First of all, notice the three great contrasts in this verse:

Wages are contrasted with gift.

Sin is contrasted with God.

Death is contrasted with eternal life.

Yes, sin pays its wages. It sometimes pays some of its wages on account, by giving an installment of a little hell on earth, but this is as nothing compared with eternity, for eternity is one long pay day. The wages that sin pays are earned.

The wages sin pays are very different from the wages that people expect.

At the time of temptation sin promises gaiety and joy, but it pays off in bitterness and gall.

Sin can promise satisfaction, but it pays off in despair.

Sometimes it promises freedom and independence, but it pays off in slavery.

It promises a lift, but pays off in wearisome burdens.

Sin will promise bright lights but pays off in eternal blackness and darkness.

Sin promises life and says "This is the life," but pays off in death.

Sin Is Deceitful

The Bible speaks quite eloquently, warning man against the deceitfulness of sin. Here are a few of the warnings from the Word of God.

"Be not deceived, God is not mocked, for whatsoever a man soweth that shall he also reap" Gal. 6:7.

"Be sure your sins will find you out" Numbers 32:23.

"The wrath of God abideth on him." Jesus said this about the man who is under sin" John 3:36.

Again the Bible warns: "When lust hath conceived, it bringeth forth sin, and sin when it is full grown bringeth death" James 1:15.

In the Old Testament we read: "Fools make a mock of sin" Proverbs 14:9.

At the last it biteth like a serpent and stingeth like an adder" Proverbs 23:32.

"The wages of sin is death" Romans 6:23.

These are only a few of the warnings about sin and its deceitfulness. These warnings are not especially for the "skid row" in a major city. These warnings reach out and touch everyone of us. Whether you are a sweet-smelling sinner or a bad-smelling sinner makes no difference to God. Sin pays its wages and there is never lack of employment in that realm. Even if work is hard to find elsewhere, you can always find employment in sin. But, praise God, this is not the end of the story!

"But the Gift of God is eternal life through Jesus Christ our Lord."

Let us look at this portion of the verse which is in contrast to the wages of sin.

The Revised Version does not just say "the gift of God" but it says "the free gift of God," and this is important. What is a gift? As it is used here, a gift is something that is free, that cannot be earned or deserved or bought. It is a gift which no man can claim as his rightful possession. Only a free gift is in the realm of Grace.

A gift is the very opposite of a wage. The worst insult that a man can offer God is to try to buy or earn salvation or a way to heaven. We live in a world where people believe that you don't get anything for nothing. This is wrong. The best things of life are free. You cannot buy them or earn them.

A mother's love is free. You can't buy it, neither can you earn it.

The privilege of being born in America is free. You cannot earn it or buy it and you did nothing to deserve it.

The air that you breathe is free and you can't buy that either.

The light of the sun and its warmth is freely given.

It is so with the salvation of God, and with Eternal Life. It is the free gift of God. It cannot be earned or deserved or bought in any way.

You may as well try to buy light from the sun as to try and earn Eternal Life. The sun gives her light. All you have to do is come out of the darkness into the light. The atmosphere gives its air. All we have to do is open our lungs and breathe.

God has provided salvation for every man, woman and child just as He has provided air for every one that breathes. It can only be received as a free gift. All that is necessary is to turn from sin and darkness and to open your heart and receive the greatest proof of God's love, His Son; Jesus Christ, as your Saviour. In Christ you will receive the gift of Eternal Life. That is how it is in the Bible and that is how God meant it to be. Anything else is an insult to God.

The free gift of Salvation is the reason God sent His Son to become one of us. The free gift is the reason Jesus could suffer and bear the pain and humiliation of the cross when He had done no wrong. Finally, He could shout in mighty triumph, "It is finished!" or "It is paid in full!" Now eternal life is free, absolutely free.

"The wages of sin is death, *but the gift of God is eternal life.*"

Sin, as it is used here, is the deliberate choosing of a wrong course, that is, wrong according to God's Word and to your own conscience. If sin is to pay its wages, it is to give payment for work, then sin must be that work which deserves the payment. This is not speaking of sin as an accident but as a deliberate and willful choice.

Sin is always in the realm of the will. The man who sinned yesterday knows good and well that he did not have to do it. I grant that there may be tendencies within him that make it difficult for him to resist. But, if he will be perfectly honest with himself he knows that the sin he committed was by choice of his own will.

We may have expected the Scripture to say, "The wages of sin is death, but the result of a holy life is Eternal Life," but it does not. Do you know why? It is because the only alternative to sin and guilt and its consequence is God doing something. Only God can help. Man chooses either God or sin, never both of them, as a course of life.

Please notice now that it does not say, "The wages of sin is death, but the outcome of reformation shall be life." That does not work, for our past sins still bring death.

Nor does it say, "The turning over a new leaf shall be life." Or: the observances of a religious ordinance or the uniting with a church shall be life." The only remedy for sin is with God. The only answer to sin is God.

What then is the remedy? In II Corinthians we read, "For God made him to be sin for us, who knew no sin, that we might be made the righteousness of God in him." This then is the free gift of God, through Jesus Christ our Lord. God has made this gift possible through the death of His Son on the cross. It was on the cross that Jesus paid the penalty for our sins.

As we look at the full meaning of this verse, we behold there the wonderful love and grace of our Lord. Isn't it wonderful to know that He is your Saviour? Isn't it glorious to live for Him, to praise Him, to live in fellowship with Him and to tell others of Him? Paul had many earthly trials but he exclaimed, "I reckon that the sufferings of this present time are not worthy to be compared with the glory which shall be revealed in us."

We also see in this verse the awful responsibility of choice which faces every one of us. One of these two courses is open to us, sin and death, or God and Eternal Life. There is no neutral ground, once you know God's will. A person comes to God, yields to Him, accepts Christ, God's appointed Saviour, as Lord. All this may be done in a blundering stumbling way but God understands and receives every honest decision. That is the beginning, the New Birth!

It is the changed attitude of the soul to God which counts, more than the outward things of religion.

For Further Study

The first evidence of God's wrath   Genesis 2:17
God's wrath as seen in the Judgment of the Flood
      II Peter 2:4,5

God's wrath causes Him to destroy a cityII Peter 2:6
God's wrath in His judgment upon Israel in the
    wilderness   Hebrews 3:7-11
God's wrath upon sin as seen in the death of His Son
                                         Romans 8:32

To many, Jesus Christ is:
    only a grand subject for a painting,
    a heroic theme for a pen,
    a beautiful form for a statue,
    or a thought for a song.

But to those who have heard His voice,
    who have felt His pardon,
    who have received His benediction,
    He is music — light — joy — hope and salvation —
    a Friend who never forsakes, lifting you up when others
    try to put you down.

There is no name like His.
    It is more inspiring than Caesar's
    more musical than Beethoven's,
    more eloquent than Demosthenes,
    more patient than Lincoln's.
The name of Jesus throbs with all life,
    weeps with all pathos,
    groans with all pains,
    stoops with all love.
Who like Jesus can pity a homeless orphan?
Who like Jesus can welcome a wayward prodigal back home?
Who like Jesus can make a drunkard sober?
Who like Jesus can illuminate a cemetery plowed with graves?
Who like Jesus can make a queen unto God out of a lost woman
    of the street?
Who like Jesus can catch the tears of human sorrow in His bowl?
Who like Jesus can kiss away our sorrow?

CHAPTER 6

The Love of God
As Seen
In His Mercy

Suggested reading: Psalm 136

According to the Bible, man has reason to praise God for His great mercy. Psalm 136, which was probably written by David, calls our attention to this wonderful attribute of God in a specific way. Although the subject of God's mercy occupies a large place in the Word of God, we find in this Psalm the quality of His mercy and certain acts which point out how He responded to the children of Israel as they were faced with dire circumstances.

The Meaning of God's Mercy

The literal meaning of mercy is that of an inward feeling of pity and compassion for someone, so much as to feel or suffer with that person. The mercy of God means therefore that it is His very nature to be tenderhearted and that He is easily moved with sympathy and compassion. Mercy is the opposite of justice, and the mercy of God means that He is moved with feelings of sympathy even though the person may fully deserve his misery.

The Mercy of God as Seen in Psalm 136

The great refrain of this Psalm is "His mercy endureth forever." For this we are to thank God with earnestness and great gratitude. First, as we read this Psalm, we notice the repetition of the words, "His mercy endureth forever." It brings to mind a choir singing a cantata and perhaps this Psalm was used as a song in the temple. We see that repetition is not always bad and that it gives strength and emphasis to the great truth of God's mercy which is actual and enduring forever. He never wearies in His pity of the sorrowing, in His protective care of the helpless, in His provision of the needy, and His pardoning grace toward the guilty; and this He does as one generation follows another generation, stumbling down the years of time, sinning, neglecting the Lord of Lords, "because He delighteth in mercy" Micah 7:18.

In verse 23 of this Psalm, we find that although God has a broad scope of mercy, He also has a personal mercy for each of us. He "remembered us in our low estate; for His mercy endureth forever." Our estate may change from day to day. Sometimes it is high, sometimes it is low. When things are going well, we should realize that all that makes us happy is from God. When our state is low because of poverty, illness, sorrow and the attacks of Satan, we aren't forgotten by God. His mercy reaches us and He will never desert us. We may think we are worthless and that God has no time for our set of problems. Our memories may fail us but God remembers and deals with us in pity.

After we have studied and absorbed from this Psalm, we should go back and read the first three verses. Three times we are admonished to "Give thanks unto the Lord."

Thank Him for who He is (verses 1-3).

Thank Him for what He is able to do (verse 4).

Thank Him for what He has done in creation (verses 5-9).

Thank Him for what He did in redeeming Israel from bondage (verses 10-15).

Thank Him for what He did in times of calamity (verses 23,24).

Thank Him for His Grace to the world at large (verse 25).

Thank Him that He remembers us, each one (verse 23).

"Give thanks unto the God of heaven, for His mercy endureth forever."

It is His mercy which causes God to be reconciled to the very worst of transgressors and to bestow blessings upon them. His *supreme* mercy is seen in His plan for redemption of sinners in which He gave His Son to be sin for us" II Cor. 5:21.

The Mercy of God as Described in the Bible

When the Holy Spirit used certain men to describe the wonder of God's mercy, He had them use a variety of adjectives such as is not found about any other subject in the whole Bible. The following are a few of them.

1. God's mercies are called "*tender*" mercies. From Psalm 51:1, "Have mercy upon me, O God, according to thy loving-kindness: according unto the multitude of thy tender mercies blot out my trans-

gressions." Also see Psalm 25:6 and Psalm 77:9.

The Hebrew word for mercy is Rachamim, which actually means the inner organs of a person. The Bible pictures this as the seat of the emotions, which is scientifically accurate. Hence the word describes the actual feeling of tender emotion which comes welling up from the inside of a person. Our English word "sympathy" comes very close to its meaning.

There is nothing hard or business-like about God's mercy. His feeling toward us is genuine, personal, and sympathetic. Not only does He have pity toward the person in trouble, but it is a tender pity that feels misery with us. His compassion is similar to that which a loving mother has for her suffering child.

The Greek words used by James to express the idea of God's feeling are "polu-spachnos-oiktirmon." These are interesting words. The word "polu" means very great, many times over, a large quantity. The word "spachnos" refers to a person's inner organs and in Greek literature is usually associated with the tender affection of the heart. Hence we get the King James translation of "very pitiful."

The word "oiktirmon" means to have compassion toward a person in trouble or misery. Taken together, these words are difficult to translate into English because in the Greek the words are piled up to express the idea of extra tenderness of feeling in the heart of God. Surely, God's mercy is *very tender* toward us.

2. God's mercy is *abundant.*

"Blessed be the God and Father of our Lord Jesus Christ, which according to His abundant mercy hath begotten us again unto a lively hope by the resurrection of Jesus Christ from the dead" (I Peter 1:3).

There is enough of God's mercy to meet our needs, with enough left over, like a cup that overflows.

We are reminded of the miracle of the loaves and the fishes. In Matthew 14:15-21 we find Jesus teaching a great crowd of people. It was in a desert place and as evening approached the desciples came and spoke to Jesus saying that He should send the people away, into the villages, so that they might eat. Then Jesus took five loaves and two fish, prayed, and gave the loaves to the disciples. The disciples gave them to the many people. They ate and all had plenty. When they gathered up the fragments that remained there were twelve baskets full. And more than five thousand had been fed. The food had been so abundant that there was much left over.

3. God is said to be *plenteous* in His mercy.

"For thou, Lord, art good, and ready to forgive; and plenteous in mercy" (Psalm 86:5). The word "plenteous" is translated "enough" in 8 different instances in the Old Testament, and "many" 190 times. The main idea is that God's mercy is enough and sufficient for man. In fact His mercy is so great that He found a way to satisfy the demands of justice through the death of Christ so that He could deliver man from his awful condition of sin.

4. God is said to be *rich* in mercy.

Notice Ephesians 2:4: "But God, who is rich in mercy, for His great love wherewith He loved us." The Greek word used is "plousios" which is translated by the word "rich" in every instance in the New Testament. Like a multi-millionaire who is never lacking in money, so God is never lacking in mercy.

When we think of riches we usually are thinking of material riches. Although God blesses us with material things, His riches refer to His heavenly riches. In Proverbs 10:22 we read "The blessing of the Lord, it maketh rich, and he addeth no sorrow with it."

So God has given us wealth in blessings and unlike material riches His blessings have no sorrows, no anxiety. Jeremiah says there is no glory in material riches (Jer. 9:23). Proverbs tells us "Labour not to be rich; cease from thine own wisdom (Proverbs 23:4). In Matthew 13:22 Jesus speaks of the deceitfulness of riches. And yet, most of us are prone to tackle a life style that is geared to our wants, instead of to our needs.

Perhaps the most well known verse about God's riches is found in Phil. 4:19. Williams gives this translation, "My God will amply supply your every need, through Jesus Christ, from His riches in glory." We certainly do not know all about the riches of God, however we have some strong hints.

We find that His riches are abundant. Psalm 52:7.

He gives us of His riches. Phil. 4:19.

He gives us richly all things to enjoy. II Tim. 6:17.

He gives us of His strength. Proverbs 18:10.

The riches of His mercy demonstrate His love. Eph. 2:4.

The earth is full of His riches. Psalm 104:24.

Jesus left all *His* heavenly riches behind when He became man. Matt. 8:20.

4. Our merciful God gives us strength and balance to follow His directions.

David was experienced in knowing his need of support when danger, temptation, and riches came his way. He was raised from the low position of a shepherd boy to become a king. He certainly loved and trusted the Lord but he found his world filled with all the powers which Satan can use to make us fail in our spiritual lives. Even though he sometimes failed miserably, the Lord used these times to show him that he must depend upon the Lord to keep him from slipping and to hold him up. He could write these words in all sincerity, "My foot slippeth; thy mercy, O Lord, held me up" (Psalm 94:18). David understood God's protective care very well. He found that the dangers of a lion, a bear and Goliath, were not as sinister as some of his own feelings.

5. God is said to *"delight"* in mercy. See Micah 7:18.

The Hebrew word used for "delighteth" (chaphets) definitely means to have pleasure in, much as we take pleasure in our children, in the daily happiness that surrounds us, in the good things of life which come our way as God delights in His children.

We should be aware that God's delight in us is conditional. There are several things that must go from us to Him to incur His delight.

(1) We find that His delight is linked with love. Deut. 10:15.

(2) It is linked to our obedience. "Hath the Lord as great delight in burnt offerings and sacrifices as in obeying the voice of the Lord? Behold, to obey is better than sacrifice. (I Sam. 15:22).

(3) His delight is linked to that special communion we have with the Lord. It is our own tender and trustful feeling we give Him. It is the element in our relationship to God which makes obedience easy. "I will delight to do thy will, O my God: yes, thy law is within my heart" (Psalm 40:8).

(4) God delights in an upright life.

Proverbs speaks so plainly, "They that are of a froward heart are an abomination to the Lord; but such as are upright in their way are his delight." This speaks of the Christian character with the will being tempered to "I will do the right thing" as opposed to "I will do the wrong thing." See Proverbs 11:20.

(5) Speaking honestly delights the Lord. Proverbs 12:22.

(6) God delights in the prayers of the upright person. Proverbs 15:8.

How does God show His delight in us?

First, He promises rewards. "Delight thyself in the Lord and He shall give thee the desires of thine heart." Psalm 37:4.

Secondly, He promises blessings (Isa. 58:14), one of which is a life of satisfaction. We already know that "things" do not bring lasting satisfaction. And no matter what our accumulation of possessions, some day we will leave it all behind. There is much more satisfaction in knowing His ways, knowing how to approach Him in prayer, knowing the meaning of the days we set aside to worship Him with others. To receive and know His Son is our greatest blessing.

Biblical Demonstrations of God's Mercy

1. God's mercy is demonstrated by His changing of man's plans.
We are all familiar with the story of Lot and Sodom. (Gen. 19:16.) Lot loved Sodom so much that although he had been warned by God that He would destroy the city, he couldn't make up his mind to leave. We are told that he lingered.

In Florida, occasionally we are threatened with a hurricane. The weather service begins to send out warnings as soon as danger approaches. "If you are on an island, please leave. We are closing the bridges. If you are in a mobile home, seek shelter in your community shelter." They repeat it over and over. And some residents are just like Lot. They linger until they have to be moved by helicopters. And even then, some will not go.

Now God could have said of Lot, "Well, it serves him right. I have warned him and have had nothing but trouble with him. Now he will have to suffer the consequences." But God has a tender heart toward even the most stubborn, so God's messengers took hold of Lot and practically carried him from Sodom. Our merciful God is like that. Sometimes we would actually be willing to lose our souls over something, but God, in mercy, takes it away from us while we still linger. Many of our earthly calamities are actually the work of God, dealing with us in love and mercy.

One of the great gospel singers of our time was on his way to being recognized in Hollywood. He knew the gospel and had realized what God's will was for him. But he "lingered" thinking of fame and fortune, contrasting that with the life of a gospel singer. But while he lingered, he contracted tuberculosis and spent the next eighteen months in a sanatorium. There he had time to reflect, pray and yield his heart to God. He thanks God for that experience of ill health. God changed his plans.

God's Mercy Is Illustrated by the Potter and the Broken Vessel

Even Jeremiah did not fully understand the mercy of God. So God gave him an object lesson. Jeremiah had a surprise when the potter instead of throwing the marred vessel on the waste heap, picked up the clay and after working over it gently, put it back on the wheel to make it into another vessel. Read Jeremiah 18:1-6.

God has always been in the "recycling business." Abraham, Jacob, Jonah, Peter, all failed Him miserably; but these men, instead of being relegated to the dump, were given another chance. This is the kind of God who loves us and who deals with us in mercy. Although we disappoint Him often, He puts the clay back on the wheel and makes us into another vessel. This illustration also shows us the wonderful patience of God as He shows mercy toward us. Like every form of art much patience is required of those who perform the actual work. It is interesting that the potter worked with clay or earth. It was God who used earth to form man in the beginning. The lesson of the "potter and the wheel" is to show us how patient, how merciful God really is.

In Exodus, chapter 34 we have another illustration of the "gracious" mercy of God. Moses had lost his temper and broken the first two tablets which held the Ten Commandments. "And the Lord said unto Moses, hew thee two tablets of stone like unto the first: and I will write upon these tables the words that were in the first tables, which thou brakest." Read the first ten verses of this chapter. In verse 6 we find a summing up by the Lord Himself. He is merciful; He is gracious; He is longsuffering; He is abundant in goodness and truth. God didn't have a copy machine. Without a word He wrote the Ten Commandments again. He is gracious. He is understanding, with the disposition to willingly try again.

There are many portions of God's Word which show us God's gracious mercy. Too many for a chapter. The book of Jonah is wonderful to study with this in mind.

God's Greatest Mercy Is Demonstrated in His Gift of Salvation

"Not by works of righteousness which we have done, but *according to his mercy He saved us,* by the washing of regeneration, and renewing of the Holy Spirit (Titus 3:3-5). Also see I Peter 1:3, 4. The main idea of these verses is that the basis of our salvation is not our good works or our good character, but God's great mercy, which caused Him to provide a remedy for our sin through the death of His Son.

D. L. Moody told of an old man who got up in one of his meetings and said, "I have been forty-two years learning three things." At this D. L. Moody began to listen, for he wanted to learn those three things. The first thing the man had learned was that he could do nothing toward his own salvation. The second thing he had found out was that God did not require him to do anything. And the third thing was that the Lord Jesus Christ had done it all. Salvation was finished and all he had to do was to take it.

The old man was right. God is great in mercy and is tender and gracious but one thing He cannot do — He cannot save anyone who trusts in His own works and wants to bypass Jesus Christ. This is an insult to God because He poured all His love, mercy, power and wisdom into that great sacrifice on Calvary.

The Apostle Paul asks us: "I beseech you therefore, brethren, by the mercies of God, that ye present your bodies a living sacrifice, holy, acceptable unto god, which is your reasonable service (Rom. 12:1).

Paul is giving us the practical application of God's mercy. The "therefore" is like a hinge which turns us back to what has been shown in Romans 8:1, 31-39. These are God's mercies. Here we find the basis of a surrendered life.

Is God pleased with our surrender to Him? Read Jer. 9:23-24.

This should be mentioned. God is not bound by all our religious technicalities. God looks at and knows the heart and He saves some who do not understand all about salvation, who do not understand all that is involved, not all that has happened to them. He saves some people who hold views that are unbiblical because a religious background can put ideas so strongly into a person's mind that they stay there a long time. There will be a lot of people in heaven who never had the joy of knowing they are eternally secure in Christ. God knows the heart.

All pastors remember incidents in weddings that were unusual. At this one particular wedding a young man that I loved was being married to a beautiful Christian girl. As often happens, the groom was a nervous wreck. As he attempted to say his vows, he lost his voice. He never did say "I do." He just nodded his head and looked like he wished the earth would open and swallow him. But I knew the intent of his heart. There was no fuss made over this technicality. He was already married in his heart to the woman he loved.

Our merciful God is as Jeremiah says, one who "exerciseth loving-kindness" in all His ways.

Questions for discussion:

Is God merciful to everyone?

Name seven "thanks" we should give God and explain why they are important.

What adjectives does the Bible use to explain God's mercy?

CHAPTER 7

The Love of God As Seen
In His Grace
Part One

Suggested reading: Psalm 105 and Romans 9

Amazing Grace! What a beautiful phrase! The Grace of God as it demonstrates God's love is one of the most amazing truths in the Bible. In trying to explain or define it, our speech becomes labored and our tongues begin to stammer, for our languages are too limited to give expression to the wonderfulness of God's grace.

Grace is the eternal and absolutely free favor and kindness of God by which He bestows eternal blessings upon guilty and unworthy sinners. Grace is — well, grace is Bible shorthand for all that God in His great love has planned and provided for sinful man.

God's grace is something in our lives which we should be aware of and know. In II Cor. 8:9 we read, "For ye *know* the grace of our Lord Jesus Christ, that, though He was rich, yet for your sakes he became poor, that ye through his poverty might be rich." This verse also points out to us that grace always existed and was present in the decisions of God. As we present this material an outline will be followed.

(1) Grace in the beginning.
(2) Grace in the past.
(3) Grace in the present.
(4) Grace in the future.

We realize we cannot do full justice to this great subject. We only will try to give you a new interest so that you may pursue this important Bible truth on your own.

Grace in the Beginning

In II Thessalonians 2:13 we read, "But we are bound to give thanks always to God for you, brethren beloved of the Lord, because *God hath from the beginning chosen you to salvation* through sanctification of the Spirit and belief in the truth." The phrase, "before the foundation of the world" also occurs in John 17:24 and I Peter 1:20.

When we consider the doctrine of Grace in the beginning we encounter a precious doctrine of the Bible, that of our election.

When I was a young Christian I memorized chapter 15 of John. I discovered verse 16 and the lamp of the Word began to shine with new intensity. The words "Ye have not chosen me, but *I* have chosen you," made such a difference in my confidence (I was struggling with do's and don'ts) and in my future Christian life. Up until that time, I had thought I did all the choosing. Now John 16:15 said He had chosen me. New strength and comfort came into my life. That is what election is all about. The Greek word "chose" conveys the meaning "He chose us for Himself."

We need to remember that this teaching is for the family of God. We must also realize that God never elected or chose anyone to be lost. Someone once called election a family secret. It should not be a secret even though sometimes it has suffered from distortion. The amazing fact is that this part of grace happened before the foundations of the world.

A key word in this doctrine is "chose." The marriage ceremony gives us a little picture of two people being chosen for a new life. There is a separation involved from others to someone else, from old loves to a new love, from an old life to a new life. It is much the same with election. God chose us in the very beginning and now we are separated unto Him to be in His keeping.

Before we get puffed up about all this, let us remember that God has perfect foreknowledge. He simply looks down the eras of time and knows what each person will do. Amazing grace!

Grace in the Garden

The first five chapters of Genesis contain a wealth of spiritual events. We cannot deal with all of them but there is one incident in the garden which shows us the wonderful grace of God. We all realize that Adam and Eve failed their first test of obedience. God in His grace had given them a free will. He had placed them in a perfect environment. And then catastrophe! Suddenly they realized something about themselves that was new to their understanding. They were naked (Gen. 3:7). It must have been a shock because it is mentioned so explicitly. Their response was to make aprons of fig leaves and cover themselves. In the perfect climate of the garden fig leaves would have been sufficient covering but now Adam and Eve would have to leave the garden and physically endure many new problems. Then God performed an act which was filled with His grace and love. "For Adam also and for his wife did the Lord God make coats of skins, and clothed them (Gen. 3:21). God made a covering for His erring pair because He still loved them. This is the first time that the shedding of blood is mentioned and it is in connection with a covering. Later God provided another covering for sinful man. "And he (Jesus) is the propitiation for our sins, and not for ours only, but also for the sins of the whole world (I John 2:2). Also check Romans 3:25 and I John 4:10. As we begin to know about God's grace we discover that all his motives and also His actions are a result of His grace and love. We find:

1. God's grace is given to us. I Peter 5:5.

God is the supreme giver. "Every good and perfect thing cometh down from the Father above (James 1:17). He *gives* His grace. Grace is not a gift from governments or kings for these sometimes persecute the godly. Grace cannot come from the world, for in this world we have tribulation. Grace is only from God and He is a liberal giver. James 4:6 specifically states that "He giveth more grace . . ". In other words the grace we receive is a gift, undeserved and unearned. In His giving of grace God is not only liberal, He is practical. He knows every need and considers what is best for us. (Phil. 4:19). Also Matt. 6:8 and Luke 12:30.

2. God's grace is the source of peace.

True peace cannot exist without the grace of God. Paul in his letter to the churches used such salutations and farewells as "Grace to you and peace from God our Father, and the Lord Jesus Christ (Romans 1:7)., "Grace be unto you, and peace. . . . . .(I Cor. 1:3)., also see I Cor. 1:2, Galatians 1:3. Notice that in the wording grace precedes peace. Even when peace eludes us as we have disquietness in our souls, grace is present. But we cannot have peace apart from grace.

3. God's grace is omnipresent in our lives.

He pours His grace into our new walk as Christians (Romans 9:38,39). His grace is in our prayer life (Romans 9:26); in our physical and spiritual strength during trials (II Cor. 12:9). His grace is even present in our entrance into heaven (I Cor. 3:22,23).

4. Grace determines our salvation.

As we see God's great love and grace we begin to dismiss our thoughts of merit or claims for salvation. The Word of God has declared that our salvation is freely given by the grace of God. It is only accomplished by the eternal favor and love of God for those who are both guilty and unworthy. See Titus 2:11 and Eph. 2:5.

Grace in the Past

As with anyone of us, there was nothing in Israel that would make that nation expecially deserving of God's Grace. For four thousand years God led them, chastened them and put up with them. Why? It is all of grace, God's undeserved and undeservable favor.

A number of years ago I had a Jewish neighbor who became very interested in the "comings and goings" that took place in our home. Eventually, she attended our church, began to read Christian material and it was quite apparent that she was intrigued by Christianity. Then her father came to visit and loud voices could be heard in an argument. He was furious over her new spiritual interest even though he had not attended temple meetings for many years.

"Abraham!" he exploded. "Well, I'll tell you about him. He was a weakling, couldn't hunt or do anything except sit outside the door of his tent and think. One day, he thought, 'I will be great! How can I be great? Well, I'll start a new religion, so he did. That's where all this nonsense originated'". That was his explanation of the Jewish nation.

God has a different story. In Deut 7:6-8 He said, "For thou art an holy people unto the Lord thy God: the Lord thy God hath chosen thee to be a special people unto himself, above all people that are upon the face of the earth. The Lord did not set his love upon you, nor choose you, because ye were more in number than any other people; for ye were the fewest of all people: But because the Lord loved you. . ." Deut. 26:18-19. "And the Lord hath avouched thee this day to be his peculiar people, as he hath promised thee, and that thou shouldst keep all his commandments; And to make thee high above all nations which he hath made, in praise, and in name, and in honour; and that thou mayest be an holy people unto the Lord thy God, as he hath spoken."

Deut. 28:9-10. "The Lord shall establish thee an holy people unto himself, as he hath sworn unto thee, if thou shalt keep the commandments of the Lord thy God, and walk in his ways. And all the people of the earth shall see that thou art called by the name of the Lord; and they shall be afraid of thee."

These three sections of scripture surely make it plain that even before Abraham, God had chosen a special people, a nation, to be different and apart from all other peoples. He would deal with them as individuals but also as a nation. The relationship would be close. The Lord told Moses to tell Pharaoh "Thus saith the Lord, Israel is *my son,* even my firstborn. And I say unto thee, let my son go that he may serve me: and if thou refuse to let him go, behold, I will slay *thy* son, even thy firstborn" (Ex. 5:22,23). Such grace and love caused the Psalmist to exclaim in a song of praise, "He hath not dealt so with any nation" (Psalm 147:20). Israel is a nation chosen of God! God has forever identified himself with Abraham, Isaac, and Jacob and their many descendants. It is a precious relationship. It is a relationship involving closeness, protection, dependence and security. In particular the King of Israel was to be a special son—which helps us understand Jesus' claim that He was the "Son of God." The word "son" in its deepest meaning was "king." As God's Son He was indeed a king.

God after choosing Israel entered into special agreements or covenants with its people. There was only one reason for this choosing and for the covenants. "The Lord did not set his love upon you, nor choose you, because ye were more in number than any people; for ye were the fewest of all people: *But because the Lord loved you.* Deut. 7:7-8.

The facts were:

1. Israel was not a mighty nation.
2. They were not an especially intelligent people.
3. They were not exceptional in looks or disposition.
4. They were just as undeserving as we are.

The greatness of God's grace is sometimes incomprehensible but let us remember that He also set His love upon us, that He chose us and the above facts pertain also to us.

A New Identity For Israel

In the father-son relationship, Israel was chosen to represent God here on earth. Israel was to be a "holy people." Since holiness denotes separation from sin and dedication to God, Israel was to maintain a new inner and outer identity. Israel was to bring glory to God, a new and separate nation which was dedicated in all her ways to the only true God. God had declared them holy (Deut. 14:2). As we sadly review the history of Israel we see how many times she forgot her holiness and her behaviour as a nation brought sorrow to God. There were the extremes. We hear them singing after God had taken them through the Red Sea, "Who is like unto thee, O Lord, among the Gods: Who is like thee, glorious in holiness, fearful in praises, doing wonders?" (Ex. 15:11). And then again "Her priests have violated my law, and have profaned mine holy things; they have put no difference between the holy and the profane, neither have they shown difference between the unclean and the clean, and have hidden their eyes from my sabbaths, and I am profaned among them" (Ezekiel 22:26).

God so graciously warned them of the results of disobedience, See Deut. 29:16-29. He told them of the wonders of obedience—"if thou shalt hearken unto the voice of the Lord thy God, to keep his commandments and his statutes which are written in this book of the law, and *if* thou turn unto the Lord thy God with all thine heart, and with all thy soul" (verse 10). The turning was never complete. But God in His love and grace never declared Israel hopeless and cast her off. See Romans 11:1,2.

As to her identity, Romans 9:4 gives us a list of grace given gifts God gave to His chosen people. Listed, they are: the adoption, the glory, the covenants, the law, service of God, the promises and the fathers (Abraham, Isaac and Jacob). Israel received a shower of grace and love.

All this was to signify that they were to be a "holy people" set apart unto God. Each time we read "holy" in the book of Deuteronomy it applies to Israel.

Why did Israel fail in being holy? Was it lack of appreciation of all that Jehovah was doing? Was it lack of humility? Was it willfulness and a self-righteous spirit? Here is a practical lesson for all of us. Are we not guilty concerning these things? A dear old lady once quoted, "Humility is a lily which grows on the grave of pride."

Humility is certainly a Christian virtue which affects our relationship to God, ". . . Be clothed with humility; for God resisteth the proud, and giveth grace to the humble" (I Peter 5:5). The grace of God gives humility, not artificial humility but the real thing. The Apostle Paul called himself "the chief of sinners" and again "Less than the least of all sinners." Paul, as he completed his missionary journeys never asked as he approached a city, "What is the best hotel in this town?" He probably inquired about the local jail because he usually spent time there.

Micah 6:8 sums up God's blueprint for Israel. "He hath shown thee, O man, what is good; and what doth the Lord require of thee, but to do justly, and to love mercy, and to walk humbly with thy God?"

Israel, a Blessing to the World

While having a discussion with a Jewish friend, I stated that the Jews were God's chosen people.

"Chosen for what?" came the reply. In the voice and especially in the facial expression hurt and bitterness plainly showed. I thought of the Spanish Inquisition, the millions of Jews who lost their lives under Hitler. I thought of anti-semitism in our own country. The conversation suddenly ended.

It was not intended that Israel would be persecuted by any other people. Israel was chosen to be a blessing to the world and since the Word of God has proclaimed it, this blessing was to have been acknowledged. "And I will make of thee a great nation, and I will bless thee, and make thy name great; and thou shalt be a blessing. And I will bless them that bless thee, and curse him that curseth thee: and in thee shall all families of the earth be blessed. (Gen. 12:2,3). "And in thy seed shall all the nations of the earth be blessed, because thou hast obeyed my voice (Gen. 22:18).

The nation of Israel has been a blessing. The Old and New Testaments, written by Jews, has preserved for us the knowledge of the one true God. The Ten Commandments strongly influenced the laws of our nation. The great heroes of the Bible have been examples to us and our children. The Apostles gave their lives for their faith in Christ. Every early Christian until the conversion of Cornelius was a Jew. The Catacombs and Coliseum in Rome tell a terrible story of the plight of the early Christians who held to their faith. Other than spiritual knowledge, the Jew has made great contributions in the fields of science, medicine, astronomy and mathematics.

The greatest blessing is that as Jesus says, "Salvation is of the Jew" (John 4:22). God chose this nation to give us our Saviour, the Lord Jesus Christ. He was born a Jew as far as His humanity was concerned (Rom. 9:5). Isaiah prophesied as to His coming. He was the "child born" and the "son given." He was also the Messiah, the Wonderful Counsellor, the Mighty God, the Prince of Peace. See Isaiah 9:6. He was both man and God, born of Israel. Note Zechariah 9:9, a wonderful prophetic verse concerning the Lord, our Saviour.

Israel, a Blessing to the Gentiles

The Apostle Paul explains in Romans 11:12,15,30 that even the national rejection of Christ by Israel is a blessing to the Gentiles. This rejection was to "riches" (12), "reconciliation with God" (15), and "mercy" (30).

Other blessings from Israel are on the agenda but are still in the future.

Questions for review or discussion:

1. What does "Amazing Grace" mean to you? Define the word "grace."
2. Explain God's election, using a key word.
3. What are four important facts about God's grace?
4. Did God's grace fail in regard to the chosen people?
5. Define "holy."
6. Mention ways that Israel has been a blessing to the world.
7. What has been the greatest blessing?
8. In the light of God's love and grace for Israel, what should be our attitude toward the Jew?

CHAPTER 8

The Love of God As Seen
In His Grace

Part Two

Suggested reading: II Cor. 12:1-10, Titus 2

Since we are going to be in the book of Titus it might be well to give a little background material. Titus was a gentile, a true and tried helper of Paul. Possibly he was a convert of Paul's early ministry. He accompanied Paul and Barnabas to Jerusalem seventeen years after Paul's conversion. We know that Titus was a pastor in Crete. Paul's letter to him was a very personal one, reminding us of his letters to Timothy. Paul had the unique ability to pour out his heart and get it all down on paper. In this little book he had much to say about many things but underlying the practical we find the wonderful theme of God's grace, which was ever present in the mind of Paul.

The Believer — a Mirror of God's Grace

Surely, the doctrines of God are never fairer than when they are seen embodied in the lives of spirit-filled believers. The believer may by his life adorn or beautify the doctrine of God. ". . .that they may *adorn* the doctrine of God our Saviour in all things" (Titus 2:10). This is an exciting possibility. His people may add beauty and luster to the Word of God. Perhaps you will appreciate the meaning of this word "adorn" if you see how it is used in other places in the Bible. In Revelation 21:2 we read, "And I, John, saw the holy city, new Jerusalem, coming down from God out of heaven, prepared as a bride, adorned for her husband." Also see Isaiah 61:10.

All brides are beautiful on their wedding day. Much preparation and expense goes into a beautiful wedding dress. But there is more than this. Every bride wants to look perfect. The "adornment" has an inner motive—to present herself as lovely as is possible. There is the inner glow of happiness which can transfigure the plainest person. Even so may our lives, when led by the spirit of God, make the doctrine of God beautiful. Such adornment is part of the gift of God's love and grace. Lest we think of this gift of God's grace as being outward and ostentatious, consider I Peter 3:3-5 and Gal. 5:22,23. Here we find the adornment of a meek and quiet spirit, love, joy, peace, long-suffering, gentleness, goodness, faith, self-control. All of these produce beauty in the Christian life and so adorn the doctrine of Grace.

The epistle of Paul to Titus was originally written to guide Titus in pastoring the church on the island of Crete. An older Paul had seen the power of the Gospel at work under all sorts of circumstances, and he was absolutely sure it worked, wherever Christ was given the opportunity. The churches of Crete had all kinds of people in them, rich and poor, masters and slaves, educated and unlearned, providing a natural climate for many problems that would tax the wisdom of a young pastor. Titus 1:12-16 gives us a terrible picture of the Cretans, summed up by "They profess that they know God, but in works they deny him, being abominable, and disobedient, and unto every good work reprobate (verse 12)." Having made this statement, Paul proceeds to present God's side of the foundation, the nature, and the hope of a beautiful Christian life, one which truly adorns the doctrines of Christ our Saviour.

First, Paul states "For the grace of God that bringeth salvation hath appeared to all men." (Titus 2:11) Jesus Christ is the embodiment of God's grace. The grace that took its rise in the councils of eternity, found its fullest expression in the experience of calvary. There all that was in the heart of God broke though the mists of sin, much like the sun breaks through fog and rain and floods the earth with light and warmth. Grace appeared in the person of Jesus Christ who died to atone for man's sin when "God was in Christ reconciling the world unto himself, not charging their trespasses unto them . . ." II Cor. 5:19,21.

Paul also states that the grace of God appeared in order to bring salvation to all men. This means *all* men, even those despicable Cretans. God's salvation is by grace, and it is for all men without distinction of race, color, nation or social standing. This is glorious and wonderful truth. This is the basis of missionary endeavor. We must forever emphasize that salvation is by grace, is the Lord's doing, from start to finish, and that any thought of helping it by human goodness or worthiness or even earnest works is an insult to God.

The School of God's Grace

The grace of God is our teacher (Titus 2:12). The word "teaches" actually means "training." It includes the thought of discipline when necessary. The word is most often translated "to chasten" and "to instruct." God's grace trains us, puts us through school as children of God, in the process of our becoming full grown, mature Christians.

There are several important areas of life in which God's grace teaches us. The negative aspect of His teaching is that the believer should deny, that is, he should denounce, turn away from, have no connection with ungodliness and worldly lusts.

Ungodliness means leaving God out of your life, out of your thinking, out of your planning. It means to follow your own will and desires instead of God's will. It can best be defined as a "self-life" instead of the "Christ-life." God's grace draws us to yield and surrender our lives to Him. Jesus said, "If any man will come after me, let him deny himself, and take up his cross and follow me (Matt. 16:24).

God's grace also teaches us to deny worldy lusts. This concerns the passions and desires which are both produced by and provided for in the world but which win and wean us away from the Lord. Some are evil in themselves. Others become evil only when they take us away from the Lord. For instance, the passion of gambling is evil in itself. But the enjoyment of a boat ride on a lake is not evil in itself. It becomes evil when it occupies the heart to where it draws us away from the Lord as is the case so often on Sunday. God's grace instructs us that we should turn away from any lust that pulls us away from God. And only the grace of God can accomplish this.

Three Areas of Life in Which Grace Teaches Us

1. We should live "soberly." (Titus 2:12)

This sober living has no relationship to sadness or sourness, a long face, or unhappiness. It simply means that we should live in consciousness of the fact that this is our one and only opportunity to glorify God, as we represent Him in the world. We are to take our vocation as the children of God seriously, for He is depending on us, more than we will ever know this side of heaven.

2. We should live "righteously." This has to do with life as it relates to our fellowmen. "No man liveth unto himself." There are ties that bind us to people. We must be careful that Satan does not use us as a stumbling block. Our lives are to be right, or righteous toward others. We must treat people in a Christ-like manner, and do so consistently. God's grace instructs us to live that we may attract others to Christ.

3. We are to live "Godly."

This speaks of life with regard towards God. Godliness is a word which Paul uses over and over. Godliness is that poise of the spirit, that attitude of the soul which expresses itself in being greatly devoted to God and to His interests. It means being ever conscious of His presence. It means a yielded life and will to Him and His Holy Spirit, until the will of God is the first consideration of life. God's grace continually teaches us, trains us as children to live a life that turns from self to the Lordship of Jesus Christ.

Immediately we recognize the fact that this is really a superhuman life which we are not capable of living in our own strength. Grace teaches us that we "should live worthy of the vocation wherewith we are called" (Eph. 4:1), "that we are to walk in love" (Eph. 5:2), and that "we should walk in the light as He is in the light" (I John 1:7). That "we should show forth the praises of Him who hath called us out of darkness into His marvelous light" (I Peter 2:9). Yes, Grace teaches us that we "should walk even as He walked" (I John 2:6), and to love one another as He loved us" (John 13:34).

All this is impossible with man, and God knew it well. That is why He sent the Holy Spirit to live within us and to be our divine enablement. Grace teaches us that our lives should manifest Christ and His glory, and Grace also provides the power to so live through the Holy Spirit. Grace teaches us that the very "Love of God is shed abroad in our hearts by the Holy Spirit which is given unto us" (Romans 5:5).

In other words, supernatural power is provided by the Lord to enable the christian to live as God would have us live. This is the provision of God's wonderful grace. We ruin His wonderful plan when we base a Christian life on human merit, or try to live by our own efforts. It is not our efforts with God helping us, but it is our giving up and recognizing Him in our lives, and then yielding to Him.

It is one of the saddest facts of our times that most Christians are almost totally unaware of this gracious provision of God for us. People are striving to attain the high standards of a Christian life asked for in God's Word in their own strength, with tragic results. This often leads to quiet hypocrisy or despondency. God has the enabling power which is fully equal to the requirements of God for Holy living. This is what Paul meant when after thirty years of the most strenuous endeavor to carry the Gospel of God's grace to the world in the face of Satanic opposition, he cried out with supreme confidence, "I can do all things through Christ which strengtheneth me" (Phil. 4:13). He knew the grace of God. He believed God. He recognized Christ in his life, and availed himself of the provision of God.

God's Grace in Suffering

Before we enter into this explanation, it would be well to read of the experience of Paul as he relates it in II Cor. 12:1-6. "The man" refers to Paul himself. Paul humbly tells of one of the most sacred moments of his life. He states that it happened 14 years before the writing down of this experience. This would put it about the time when he was traveling as a missionary in the cities of Iconium, Derbe, and Lystra. Acts, chapter 14, gives us this history. Many Bible students have believed that Paul's visit to paradise actually took place during his stoning at Lystra (verse 19). These students believe that while his body was lying on the ground, apparently dead, his spirit was caught up into paradise. Though this view may be correct, no one can say so with certainty because we have not been told. But we know Paul was caught up into the spirit world. He could not even tell whether he was in the body or whether his pesence was there in the spirit. It was undoubtedly a real experience and a very wonderful experience. What he saw and heard so far transcended the things of our earthly sphere that he found human language incapable of conveying to others the glory that had been revealed to him.

Paul says he was caught up into "the third heaven" (verse 2). The first heaven is our atmospheric heaven. Beyond that is the starry heaven. Beyond the sphere of the stars and planets there is another world of spiritual wonder where Christ is and where the saints and angels are with Him. It is the unseen world which Paul calls the third heaven. This world is just as real as our own seen world.

Paul also describes this place as "paradise" (verse 4). The word "paradise" is found only three times in the New Testament. It is a Persian word, written in the Greek language and meaning "a royal garden." Its primary meaning is a most beautiful royal garden with all kinds of flowers and trees and fruit and is generally a place of wonderful beauty and rest. Jesus used this word when speaking to the thief on the cross who begged to be remembered when Christ came into His kingdom. See Luke 24:43. It is a descriptive reference to the unseen world beyond our physical sphere which is the abode of those who have gone on to be with the Lord.

Here Paul heard unspeakable words and saw things beyond description.

Paul Is Given a Thorn in the Flesh

"And lest I should be exalted above measure through the abundance of the revelations, there was given to me a thorn in the flesh, the messenger of Satan to buffet me, lest I should be exalted above measure." II Cor. 12:7. Here we have an abrupt change. The scene of Paul's experience is suddenly changed from paradise to pain. This is often the case in Christian experience. Where there is a mountain top, there is a valley nearby. The experience of Paul's thorn in the flesh has many valuable lessons for us today.

1. The nature of the thorn.

Few subjects in the Bible have called for more speculation than the nature of Paul's thorn. Some think that it was some particular spiritual suffering or temptation that Paul endured. Others have had an idea of epileptic fits. Many have concluded that he had serious eye trouble, and this thought may have support from certain expressions which we find in Paul's letter. All of this is merely conjecture. One thing is sure, this thorn afflicted Paul's physical body. See Gal. 4:13. The word "thorn" is a poor word since a thorn can be very small. The word "thorn" means a sharpened stick which would constantly prick the flesh, like a sliver under the fingernail which cannot be reached.

There was also the mental agony as Paul persisted in prayer (three times in Hebrew meaning continuously) as his wishes were denied. We can understand the desolation of spirit which accompanied his suffering. When we suffer physically Satan uses the opportunity to "buffet" us.

The very fact that the Scripture is silent as to the nature of this thorn is proof that the truth contained in Paul's relation of this personal experience is to be applied to that particular thing each one of us may have to overcome. If we had been told precisely what the thorn was, we would immediately conclude that we must have that identical problem for God's grace to be sufficient. I am glad that I do not know what that thorn was as now I feel free to apply the same truths to my own experience.

2. The source of the thorn.

In II Cor. 12:7 the words "there was given to me" seem to indicate that the Lord himself had permitted this suffering to come to Paul. It may be difficult to bring ourselves to believe that God can be, and is, associated with suffering; nevertheless such is the case. It is by His permissive will that suffering comes our way. David said, "It is good for me that I have been afflicted; that I might learn thy statutes" (Psalm 119:71). At the same time Paul affirms that the thorn is the messenger of Satan, so that while it was God-given we are reminded that it is our adversary, the Devil, who is anxious to hurt us. He always has been and always will be the agent of everything that is in this world in the way of suffering.

Though we will never be able, in our present state, to understand the great mystery of suffering, we must keep in mind that even though Satan is anxious and willing to afflict us, God will overrule him and will use even human suffering for our good and for His glory as was the case with Paul's thorn.

3. The purpose of the thorn.

The purpose of the thorn as far as Satan was concerned was doubtless to buffet or pound Paul with pain, and so to discourage him. But as far as God was concerned the purpose was to keep Paul from being exalted, or lifted up, with self-esteem and pride to where God could not use him. "Lest I should be exalted above measure." Verse 7. The one thing God cannot use in man is pride and self-sufficiency. Notice, Paul speaks of being exalted "above measure." No normal human being could help being exalted over such an experience as the apostle had and there would be no sin in being "lifted up." But the danger was, and the sin involved was that he would become "exalted above measure." In other words God provided a fence at the top of the precipice rather than an ambulance at the bottom. To save Paul from falling, God permitted a thorn in his flesh. In it we see the wisdom of Almighty God. The worst enemy of the Christian life, especially with successful people, is pride. The hardest thing to get rid of in life is pride.

There is usually someone who helps us control our feelings of pride. A young pastor stood at the door after the morning service, receiving many compliments on his message. An elderly Christian lady came by and said sincerely, "Pastor, I want to thank you for that message."

"Oh, don't thank me," replied the glowing pastor, "just thank the Lord."

"Well, " replied a soft little voice, "I considered that, but it wasn't quite that good."

Paul's Experience With God in Prayer (II Cor. 12:8-13)

1. Paul's prayer (verse 1).

"For this I besought the Lord thrice, that it might depart from me." Plainly speaking, this means that Paul prayed for healing. It was a normal, natural reaction to pain. Since he was a man who believed in prayer he asked the Lord to take away the source of his suffering.

In failing to measure up to the standards maintained by Paul, we often fail to enjoy a like fruitful experience and remain in a state of rebellion. Sometimes we are not willing to accept the fact that God has heard our plea but that it does not suit His purpose to respond and deliver us. Consequently our ears are not attuned to His voice and we do not hear Him saying to us that His strength will be perfect in us if only we will press on and trust in Him completely. At times we complain instead of conforming to His perfect, though seemingly undesirable will and we will not and do not say "amen" to His perfect judgment.

2. God's answer to Paul's prayer.

"And He said unto me, My grace is sufficient for thee: for my strength is made perfect in weakness." God did answer Paul's prayer but not in the way Paul first desired it. God did not remove the thorn, but rather gave grace sufficient for the bearing of the suffering.

We should notice that the words of the Lord, "My grace is sufficient for thee," express a fact rather than just a promise. To overcome in affliction is better than to be delivered from it.

To illustrate this precious truth: Some sixty years ago a promising young minister in England had lost his little daughter in death. Heartbroken and crushed by the loss he was in an agony of suffering and darkness. One day he went into his study to prepare a sermon. He dropped down on his knees and cried out to God for help and comfort and deliverance. He prayed, "O Lord, make thy grace sufficient for me in this hour of sorrow and darkness." Opening his eyes he saw on the wall a text reading, "My grace is sufficient for thee." The word "is" was in different colored ink from the other words. A glorious truth stood out. The young man rose to his feet and started thanking and praising the Lord. He saw that he had been asking God to make a fact of something that was already a fact. He could now say in joy and thanksgiving, "Lord, I do not need to ask thee to make Thy grace sufficient for me. I praise Thee that it *is* sufficient."

The thorn was also to be a means for the displaying of God's strength. The Lord said, "My strength is made perfect in weakness." It is when we fully realize our own weakness that we come to rely upon God's grace. Only then can God do with us what He wants to do. In this manner the thorn in the flesh served to prove to Paul his own weakness and God's strength at one and the same time. His personal inability to cope with the difficulty forced upon him the necessity to seek assistance apart from self. Thus he was driven to the only fountainhead of invincible strength, even Jesus Christ himself.

3. Paul's changed attitude toward the thorn. (verse 9b-13).

The key to suffering is our attitude toward it. Paul's attitude became "Therefore I take pleasure in infirmities, in reproaches, in necessities, in persecutions, in distresses for Christ's sake; for when I am weak, then am I strong" (verse 10). He considered his ailment not as a hindrance now in life, but as a channel of God's strength. The verses indicate that Paul was glad because of his thorn—not because of the suffering in itself, but because it was "for Christ's sake." Most gladly does he glory in his weakness and ailments as he sees them in the light of God's grace. Apart from all this he might have been tempted to trust in his own puny strength which would have brought forth nothing. Through that thorn he was able to realize the very height of his ambition, to present his life strengthened by the power of Christ which rested upon him.

Was Paul's thorn worthwhile? As we look back on Paul's ministry we say a thousand times, "yes."

His Future Grace to Israel

The whole Bible tells us that God is not through with Israel. Paul asked, "Has God cast away his people?" The answer, "God has not cast away His people whom he foreknew" (Romans 11:1-2). "For finding fault with them he saith, Behold the days come, saith the Lord, when I will make a new covenant with the house of Israel and with the house of Judah: Not according to the covenant that I made with their fathers in the day that I took them by the hand to lead them out of the land of Egypt, because they continued not in my covenant, and I regarded them not, saith the Lord. For this is the covenant that I will make with the house of Israel after those days, saith the Lord; I will put my laws in their mind, and write them in their hearts: and I will be to them a God, and they shall be to me a people" (Heb. 8:8-10; cf. Jer. 31:31-33).

Israel will be restored, God is going to gather them out of all nations to the promised land. And now they will be under God's grace. At present they seek their own righteousness. Paul's heart was heavy when he thought about his brethren. (Romans 10:1) His prayer was that they might be saved. But he concludes, remembering the words of the prophet Elijah, "Even so, then, at this present time also there is a remnant according to the election of grace." (Rom. 11:5). Paul, himself, was an example of the remnant.

There will come a time, during the great tribulation (Matt. 24:21) when the nation of Israel will behold their Messiah and they shall mourn when they see the marks of the crucifixion in his hands. See Rev. 1:7. They will turn to Jesus Christ, the rejected Saviour, and become the greatest missionary force this world has ever known. Presently, we have an important "until" attached to the status of Israel in the world (Rom. 11:25 cf. Luke 21:24). But the day will come when Israel will rejoice in the presence of the Saviour and enjoy His wonderful grace.

The Grace of God in Its Eternal Purpose (Titus 2:14)

The grace of God in its eternal purpose is that He may have a people for His own possession. "Who gave himself for us, that he might redeem us from all iniquity, and purify unto himself a peculiar people, zealous of good works."

Here is the marvel and mystery of the grace of God in its unveiling. The Son of God who was with the Father in the measureless past of eternity, became flesh and gave Himself for us. Christ endured the pain and agony of the cross, the loneliness and friendlessness, spiritual and physical death, as He gave Himself for us. The first hint of this is found in that sad judgment scene in Eden where judgment was pronounced and the Deliverer was promised as the Seed of the woman. The final glory of this is heard in that flaming song in heaven to the Lamb as revealed in the book of Revelation. "Thou art worthy to take the book, and to open the seals thereof: for thou wast slain, and hast redeemed us to God by thy blood out of every kindred, and tongue, and people and nation." (Rev. 5:9)

Jesus Christ not only redeemed us, but ever lives to purify us. Read Eph. 5:25-27. This present purification is accomplished through the laver of the Word of God. That is why we need to draw ever nearer to God's Word in our interest and for all our spiritual information. Jesus prayed, "Sanctify them through thy truth, thy word is truth."

God desires a people for His own possession. That is the meaning of the term "peculiar." God wants a people who have been saved out of this world, who belong to Him by choice, upon whom He can bestow all His love and care, and who will love Him back. These He will present in a future time, in a glorified state, when they shall be like Him, and then He will be the first among many Brethren. O, the marvels of God's grace! We are the Lords and He is ours, and all things are ours in Him. He lives in us and we are His own people.

Questions to Consider

1. Which is more important, outer or inner adornment?

2. In becoming a mirror of God's grace, what three areas are important?

3. Why did God not remove "the thorn" from Paul?

4. In what two ways does God answer our prayers?

5. What affect does watching for the Lord's return have in our daily lives?

6. Considering God's Word, what should be our attitude toward Israel?

7. Does the sufficiency of Christ exist in all areas of life?

Chapter 9

The Love of God As Seen In His Faithfulness

Suggested Reading
Psalm 147
Psalm 100
Luke 11:1-14

"The Lord delights in those who fear him, who put their hope in his unfailing love." Psalm 147:11 (New International Version).

Faithfulness is one of the attributes of God. The Biblical meaning is that God is without failure and therefore dependable in the absolute sense, being completely worthy of all the trust that mankind may place in Him. God's faithfulness is in great contrast to the faithfulness of man. Even though a man or woman means to be faithful to a promise it is not always possible to keep that promise. Circumstances may enter in which cause the faltering of purpose. We see this in the life of Peter who said to Jesus, "Lord, why cannot I follow thee now? I will lay down my life for thy sake." John 13:37 and then in John 18:25, "And Simon Peter stood and warmed himself. They said, therefore, unto him, Art not thou also one of his disciples? He denied it, and said, I am not."

But with God, there are no circumstances beyond His control. He is faithful in an unlimited sense. When He promises something, it is as good as done. His love never fails; His faithfulness never wavers.

The Hebrew word used for God's faithfulness in the Old Testament is "Emunah", which in its root form means "that which is fastened down so that it is secure." From this word, we get the meaning of security, trustworthiness, truth, firmness, and everlasting faithfulness.

The Greek word used for God's faithfulness in the New Testament is "Pistos," which occurs in one or another form in the New Testament and is usually translated by the word "faith" or "believe." Its basic meaning is that of trusting, of committing, of having confidence in. As applied to God, it means that He is absolutely trustworthy.

The faithfulness of God is depended upon by all nature and by all life on earth. In Genesis 8:22, God promised the continued change of the four seasons. "While the earth remaineth, seedtime and harvest, and cold and heat, and summer and winter, and day and night shall not cease." Everything and everyone depends upon this promise, even that one who says there is no God. The farmer counts on it to produce that most important factor of life, our food. From the greatest star to the smallest creature, nature works in a constant rhythm which never fails. We speak of the "miracle of spring." But each change of season is a continuing miracle, setting forth the wisdom and faithfulness of the creator. This is a promise and will always be "while the earth remaineth." If anything happened to disrupt the seasons, a world-wide catastrophe would follow. See I Peter 4:19.

God, Himself, says that He is faithful, "Know therefore that the Lord, thy God, he is God, *the faithful God,* which keepeth convenant and mercy with them that love him and keep his commandments to a thousand generations." Deut. 7:9.

Consider these New Testament verses related to Deut. 7:9. See I Cor. 1:9 (He is faithful as to our calling into the fellowship of His son). Also I Thess. 5:24. And we find in II Thess. 3:3 that He is faithful to establish us, once we are called, and to keep us from evil.

God Is Said to be Faithful to Himself

"If we believe not, yet he abideth faithful; he cannot deny himself." II Tim. 2:13.

The truth emphasized here is that God will always be true to what he is and act in accordance with His character. He will not compromise with evil under any circumstances. Yet, He will not fail to act like a true father toward His own children. He cannot deny Himself; He cannot act contrary to His true nature as a faithful God. As James has said, "With him is no variableness, neither shadow of turning." James 1:17.

This is in pleasant contrast to man. We are unpredictable in our conduct, sometimes behaving more like the "old" self and then again like the "new creature in Christ." This is also in contrast to our circumstances which can change drastically and quickly. Jeremiah states in Lam. 3:22,23 "It is of the Lord's mercies that we are not consumed, because his compassions fail not. They are new every morning. *Great is thy faithfulness."*

Our circumstances undergo constant change. "Things" wear out, inflation hurts our finances, ill health undermines the joy of life, great losses and trials test our faith. These are perils we encounter, but God's love and compassion are ever new just as in His faithfulness He causes the darkness of night to be changed into the light of day.

God Is Faithful to His Word
Hebrews 10:22,23

In I Tim. 1:15 we read "This is a *faithful saying,* and worthy of all acceptation, that Christ Jesus came into the world to save sinners; of whom I am chief."

God's promise of salvation to those who trust in Christ will be kept. This is the word of our faithful God and so it becomes a "faithful saying." Satan is the master-mind of doubt concerning Jesus Christ and our salvation in Him. He suggests that God is mainly interested in the "good ones." He creates doubt as to whether God can really forgive us. The promises of God are always kept. See I John 1:9. He has said, "If we confess our sins, *he is faithful* and just to forgive us our sins, and to cleanse us from all unrighteousness."

God has given His unfailing promise to the children of God that when we confess our sins He will both forgive and cleanse us from all sin and unrighteousness. No believer should ever despair because he has miserably failed God. God has pledged in His faithfulness, no matter how serious the offence or how often it may have been committed, if confessed, it will be forgiven.

We are to come to God in full assurance, in full confidence, for we can depend on Him to keep His promise. Trusting in His faithful Word, we should never doubt the outcome of the Christian life. "But the salvation of the righteous is of the Lord; he is their strength in the time of trouble." Psalm 37:39.

God's Faithfulness Is the Source
Of Great Confidence in Prayer

In Hebrews 2:17 we read of God's Son, "Wherefore in all things it behooved him to be made like unto his brethren, that he might be a merciful and *faithful* high priest in things pertaining to God, to make reconciliation for the sins of the people."

1. God hears our prayers.

Is God listening when we pray? We have the assurance of the Word of God that God in His love for us is faithful in hearing our prayers. His ears are open to our prayers, be they great or small. "O thou that hearest prayer, unto thee shall all flesh come." Psalm 65:2. He not only hears our prayers He blesses those who pray. In Psalm 65:4, we read that He blesses the person who approaches Him in prayer. Among these were Moses, Aaron and Samuel (mentioned in Psalm 99:6) and we are told, "He answered them." Also see Isa. 58:9.

Jesus testified as to God's faithfulness in answering prayer. Standing before the tomb of Lazarus, He lifted up His eyes and said, "Father, I thank thee that thou hast heard me. And I knew that thou hearest me *always* . . ." John 11:41,42.

Consider these precious promises: Matt. 18:19, Matt. 21:22, James 5:16.

2. God answers our prayers.

The 11th chapter of Luke, 1-13, gives us three parabolic illustrations that Jesus used in answer to a request. "Lord, teach us to pray." Here we find that God is faithful in hearing and answering our prayers.

First, notice the request. This was not a request for the mechanics of prayer. It went far beyond that and was born of the manner in which Jesus prayed to His Father. The disciples saw the familiar communication (even though this was God speaking to God) they realized the depth of the bond between Father and Son; they were spiritual enough to realize that prayer is concerned with love, a relationship of the Spirit, a confidence based on truth and experience. They wanted to pray as Jesus prayed.

Jesus answered their request by using some illustrations. First He spoke of a man who did not want to be troubled by requests for help in an inconvenient time. Then we find a friend, a persistent person, who annoys his neighbor until he finally receives what he wanted. But his friend only arose because of the importunity of the man in need. "Importunas" is a Latin word, meaning troublesome. He answered the door in order to rid himself of a problem.

This Scripture has been misunderstood by many Christians who think we must come to God in prayer and agonize repeatedly until He answers us. Jesus used this illustration only as a contrast to the real facts of prayer. In His clear statements:

"And I say unto you, Ask, and it shall be given you; seek, and ye shall find; knock, and it shall be opened unto you. For every one that asketh receiveth; and he that seeketh findeth; and to him that knocketh it shall be opened" (Luke 11:9,10). Also see Psalm 99:6, Isa. 58:9, John 11:42, Isa. 59:1.

This does not mean that a prayer is not to be repeated. The Holy Spirit brings to mind our need of communication concerning our needs, our problems and our loved ones.

Verses 11,12,13 of Luke 11 show us how God answers prayer. Notice that the relationship, that of a father and child, is important. Then notice that God gives appropriate answers. His answers are not stones, serpents or scorpions but rather sustaining factors, such as, bread, fish or eggs. It is as Jesus said, "If you then, being evil, know how to give good gifts unto your children, how much more shall your Father which is in heaven give good things to them that ask Him?" Matt. 7:11. Also see Psalm 65:2-4. We can approach God in full assurance because He has promised to hear and answer our prayers.

God Is Faithful in Seeing Us
Through Temptation
(See I Cor. 10:13 and Heb. 2:17,18)

"There hath no temptation taken you but such as is common to man; but *God is faithful,* who will not suffer you to be tempted above that ye are able; but will with the temptation also make a way to escape, that ye may be able to bear it." I Cor. 10:13. See Heb. 2:17,18.

The implications of this great truth are great and far reaching so often we think that our situation is unique. When we face painful and adverse circumstances we need to know that God is faithful and will not let us go beyond His power and beyond His love. In times of great stress and temptation we sometimes feel that God is not loving us and we experience a withdrawal from Him. But He never withdraws. As David said in Psalm 23:4 "Yea, though I walk through the valley of the shadow of death, I will fear no evil; for *thou art with me;* thy rod and thy staff they comfort me." In a normal Christian life there are many valleys, many shadows, many temptations. Satan would have us believe He doesn't understand, He doesn't care, but He cares and gives us strength to bear whatever it is. I Peter 4:12,19 and I Peter 5:7.

The Faithfulness of God
Is the Basis of the Believer's Assurance

His faithfulness is our solemn guarantee of our future glory with Him. "Faithful is he that calleth you, who also will do it." I Thess. 5:24 with Rev. 21:4,5.

His faithfulness gives us complete assurance. I Cor. 1:8-9 and Phil. 1:6. Note that in II Tim. 1:12 we see the basis of Paul's assurance. "For the which cause I also suffer these things; nevertheless I am not ashamed; for I know whom I have believed, and am persuaded that he is able to keep that which I have committed unto him against that day."

Man often fails in his work. Close by there is a half finished house, the bare walls are there without the roof, weeds and trees are growing inside the walls. Someone started to build a house but something happened. Did the builder die? Did his family break up so that he no longer needed a house? Did he find it financially impossible? Here stands a tragic reminder of man's inability to always complete what he starts. Not so with God — Paul tells us in Phil. 1:6 "Being confident of this very thing, that he which hath begun a good work in you will perform it until the day of Jesus Christ."

God's Faithfulness as Seen in His Holiness

"The Lord is righteous in all his ways, and holy in all his works." Psalm 145:17.

We should give thanks as we remember His holiness. "Sing unto the Lord, O ye saints of his, and give thanks at the remembrance of his holiness." Psalm 30:4.

Holiness is among the most frequently mentioned attributes of God. This is because holiness is a very basic part of God's nature. Even as we cannot conceive of God unless He be almighty, so He cannot be God unless He is absolutely holy.

God's holiness is the glory and beauty of all His other attributes. Without His perfect holiness His other attributes would become imperfect. For instance, His justice is a holy justice because of His holiness. His law is a holy law. His wrath is a holy wrath. His love is a holy love. Without holiness behind it, His wrath would become madness, His power would become selfish, His patience would be but indulgence, and His love would be blind. His absolute holiness sanctifies them all and makes every attribute to work in perfect harmony toward God's holy purpose.

If we are to understand God's faithfulness as seen in His holiness, we must understand these principal points:

1. The meaning of the holiness of God.
2. How the holiness of God is manifested.
3. The holiness of God as manifested in His law.
4. The holiness of God as manifested in His salvation for man.

The Meaning of the Holiness of God

The principal meaning of the word "holy" means to be separated from evil. Accordingly, God is absolutely free from anything that is evil or false. He is true and perfect and pure in His person and in all His works.

"This then is the message which we have heard of him, and declare unto you, that God is light and in him is no darkness at all." (I John 1:5) See Isa. 6:2,3, Rev. 4:8 and Rev. 15:4.

God cannot do anything evil nor have any pleasure in that which is evil or false. It is true that God has a free will and can do as He pleases, but because of His holiness He can only desire to do that which is also perfect. For example, God was at liberty to create angels or man, but when He created them it was necessary, because of His holiness, to create them righteous. God was at liberty to speak to man, but when He spoke it was impossible for Him to speak that which was false. God was at liberty as to whether He would permit man to sin, but once man had sinned it was impossible for God to accept that sin or to do anything but hate and judge it.

How the Holiness of God Is Manifested

1. The Holiness of God is manifested in His creation.

Man was created in the image and likeness of God. This means man was created in perfection. "Image" may well refer to man's form, but "likeness" refers to inward quality, to the spiritual nature of man. See Genesis 1:26,27.

"And God saw everything that he had made, and behold, it was very good. (Gen. 1:31).

God created man as a perfect being without sin, but with a free will. It was not until man entered experience by the wrong door of disobedience that any sin was found in him. Immediately, God in His holiness judged the sin and the sinner, and part of that judgment is the sinful and unholy nature which became the lot of mankind. Not only man, but angels and other rational beings were created in perfect holiness. (Ezek. 28:15).

This verse refers particularly to Satan who was perfect in his ways from the day God created him until he fell the victim of ambition. This creates a problem in our minds, involving the question of how this exalted angel with a perfect nature could fall. Could it be that part of a perfect nature is a free will? But we know he did rebel and led about one-third of the angels into rebellion with him. See Jude 6.

There are three things that are plainly true about angels and the first man who sinned against God.

1. They were all created sinless and perfect.
2. In time, some of the angels and of course the first man sinned against God.
3. In each case, God was true to His holy nature and brought swift judgment upon all who sinned.

God's Holiness Is Manifested
In His Hatred of All Evil and Falsehood

A careful study of this subject will bring to light the very great emphasis which the Bible gives to God's hatred of all evil and falsehood. Consider the following passages as examples:

Habakkuk 1:13 "Thou art of purer eyes than to behold evil, and canst not look on iniquity; wherefore, lookest thou upon them that deal treacherously, and holdest thy tongue when the wicked devoureth the man that is more righteous than he?" Also see Amos 5:21-24. In these verses, the Lord speaks His mind concerning the hypocrisy of people in their religious attitudes. Notice the words with which His feelings are expressed. "I hate," "I despise," "I will not smell," "I will not accept."

In Isa. 1:11-15, the Lord tells how He feels about the outward worship that comes from sinful lives. Observe the following phrases: "I delight not," "an abomination," "I cannot away with," "Iniquity," "my soul hateth," "they are a trouble unto me," "I am weary of them," "I will hide mine eyes."

There is only one thing that God hates and that is sin in any form or fashion. Though He loves the person who sins, He always hates the sin which is the source of all misery in His creatures. We must never think for a moment that God feels any different about sin when it is committed by His own children. God's holiness cannot look upon sin without loathing and hatred. This fact makes the transaction of the Cross of Calvary all the more wonderful and man's rejection or neglect of it the more condemning. See Romans 1:18.

God's Holiness Is Manifested in His Holy Law

"Wherefore the law is holy, and the commandment holy, and just, and good." Romans 7:12.

One of the greatest proofs of the holiness of God and of the inspiration of the scripture by a holy God is the law. This law is a code of righteousness so perfect, so completely free from the prevailing philosophies and superstitions of the world at that time when it was given, so perfectly suited to the fundamental righteousness and duties of man toward God and toward his fellowman that it is even today the basis of all law and order.

This law teaches man the noblest manner of living. The life that it commands can only result in honor to God, in the happiness of the one who follows it. When we consider the fact that this perfect code was given at a time when the whole world had standards which considered such things as idolatry, sex relationship outside the bond of marriage, prostitution, etc. a necessary part of life, the holy law of God is a divine miracle. Only a loving, faithful, holy God can account for this.

Further facts about the spiritual nature of the law —

1. We read in Romans 7:14 "For I know that the law is spiritual." The laws of the world deal only with the outward acts of man. They can forbid the act of theft but never forbid the covetous desire of the unclean thought of the heart.

God's holy law forbids and condemns the evil thought and intention of the heart as much as the deed itself, because it is from the heart of man that evil deeds come forth. See Mark 7:21,22. Also Matt. 5:27,28 and Matt. 5:21,22.

2. The holiness of God is manifested in His salvation for man.

This is indeed the strongest evidence of God's holiness which remains unchangeable and which cannot look upon sin except with loathing and hatred. The sacrificial death of His Son is the basis of man's salvation. Romans 8:32. Also see II Cor. 5:21, I Peter 3:18, Isa. 53:3-6,10,11. There are other evidences of God's hatred of sin — the destruction of Sodom, the terror of the great flood, but nothing demonstrates God's hatred of sin as strongly as when we see His wrath poured out upon the sinless Son of His love. "For he hath made him to be sin for us, who knew no sin; that we might be made the righteousness of God in him." II Cor. 5:21. And when that happened, God withdrew himself in that awful hour until Jesus cried out, "My God, my God, why has thou forsaken me?" (Matt. 27:46).

3. God's holiness is seen in the sinner's justification, which is based on the death of Christ. See Romans 5:8-9 and Romans 3:23,24.

The sinner is justified when God saves him. This means that he is declared righteous. Let us again say, this justification is never based upon the goodness of man or good works, but only upon the death of Christ whose blood was shed to atone for man's sin. We are plainly taught that we must disown and distrust any righteousness or goodness of our own and receive the righteousness of God provided through the death of Christ.

4. God's holiness is seen in the believer's sanctification which is part of God's plan of salvation. See I Thess. 4:3 and John 17:17.

"To sanctify" means to set apart from sin. The words "sanctify," "saint" and "holiness" all come from the same root. After we are saved, God wants us to be set aside more and more from the practices of sin. This part of sanctification is a process, accomplished by the work of the holy spirit through the Word of God. This part of God's plan is very much in keeping with His love and faithfulness as well as His holiness. Examine John 8:11. Hear Jesus saying, "Neither do I condemn thee," and in the next breath He said, "Go and sin no more."

God's Faithfulness in His Relationships with His Children

Perhaps this is where as J. Vernon McGee says, "the rubber meets the road." This is the message we so badly need. Is God faithful to each of us and our needs? Hebrews 10:22,23 tells us that God is faithful and that we can draw near to Him with full assurance of faith. We find the Bible is filled with the faithfulness of God to many people, meeting their needs of the hour. We have:

Abraham's spiritual needs which God answered by giving him faith and courage. Gen. 22:13.

Ruth's physical need with God giving her food and direction in the fields of Boaz. Ruth 2:8,9.

Daniel in physical danger, with God delivering him from the lions. Dan. 6:22.

David prevailing over Goliath with God granting courage and direction. I Sam. 17:50.

Joseph being restored to power and position in Egypt. Gen. 41:43.

God is faithful to Israel. Romans 11:26-29, Mal. 3:6.

Lydia, being used as a new convert. Acts 16:14,15.

Rahab being honored for her faith. Joshua 6:22,23.

Mary and Martha, having their brother restored to life. John 11:43.

Peter being saved from lack of faith. Matt. 14:31.

God's faithfulness to us all in His salvation. Rom. 8:32,28.

It is of special significance that Christ should emphasize the precious promise of the wonderfulness of the conditions in Heaven with the statement that these words are true and faithful. It must be that He wanted us to be especially assured of these things so that our hope may keep us true to our calling throughout all opposition. God is faithful to us in the present and also in our future life in Heaven with Him. "And God shall wipe away all tears from their eyes; and there shall be no more death, neither sorrow, nor crying, neither shall there be any more pain; for the former things are passed away. And he that sat upon the throne said, Behold, I make all things new. And he said unto me. Write; *for these words are true and faithful.* Rev. 21:4,5.

Questions to Consider

1. What great difference do we find in the faithfulness of God and the faithfulness of man?
2. Should God's faithfulness fail, what would happen in the world?
3. Who affirmed that God always hears our prayers?
4. What is the relationship of God's holiness to His faithfulness?
5. How is God's holiness manifested?
6. Who would you add to the list of those mentioned in the study of God's faithfulness to His children?
7. What proof do we have of His eternal faithfulness?

CHAPTER 10

The Love of God As Seen In the Ministry of His Son

Suggested Reading: The Gospel of Mark

"Is not this the carpenter, the son of Mary . . ." was asked as Jesus began His public ministry. We can easily imagine the utter astonishment of His family, friends, and many others as they saw the young carpenter of Nazareth desert His trade and begin a ministry such as has never been known to man. There is no doubt that His very person was an astonishment. Although little is known of those years in the carpenter shop, we know from many witnesses much truth about the three years of His ministry. Those close to Him were amazed. Whether they understood or did not, they were seeing a revelation of God's nature — His power, His purity, His wisdom, His majesty, His greatness and His love.

In Luke 2:47 we see amazement at His understanding.

In Luke 4:32 we find astonishment at His doctrine.

In Luke 5:9 we see astonishment at His miracles.

In Luke 9:43 we see amazement at His power.

The four gospels tell us many facts which picture for us the person of Jesus Christ, God's Son. We find:

(1) He was a man of joy. "These things have I spoken unto you, that *my joy* might remain in you, and that your joy might be full. John 15:11.

We are told in Luke 10:21 that He *exulted* or rejoiced in the Holy Spirit. This word in the Greek is a very strong one and means exuberance and a joy which fills the heart to overflowing. As He proclaimed His news of salvation it is impossible to believe that He did this with a long face and a mournful spirit. He knew joy and came to share His joy. He came to conquer sin and set its captives free. To Him it was a privilege. The very sorrowful task of Calvary shed a spiritual joy upon His ministry. To think of Christ as One without great joy is to lower Him to an unreal position.

(2) He was a man of tender emotions.

We find Jesus in John 11:33-36 groaning and weeping at the tomb of Lazarus: Here we see an emotional part of Jesus' nature. It has been speculated that His groaning and tears were because He was reviewing the awful fact of death as a part of the curse of sin. Certainly, He already knew that His friend would be restored to life. But the tears and the groaning were real and had been brought about by the great sorrow which had come to His friends. They were understood as an expression of His love for Lazarus. John 11:35, 36.

That He was emotionally tender is seen in every part of His ministry. Even as His time on earth approaches an end, His compassion reached out to Mary, His mother. On the cross, His tenderness was expressed when he gave Mary into the care of John, whom He loved. John 19:26, 27. Also see His tenderness when He forgave the thief who was crucified with Him. Luke 23:43. He suffered over human distress. Mark 7:32-36, Hebrews 4:15 tells us that He is *touched* with the feeling of our infirmities (and they are many). In Mark 1:41 we see Jesus touching and healing a leper. Understanding the pangs of hunger He had compassion on a multitude of hungry people and saw that they were fed. Mark 8:2.

(3) He was a man of prayer.

"Since Christ was God, why must He pray?
By Him all things were known and made,
Omniscient and omnipotent,
Why need He ever ask for aid?
Ah! but He put His glory by,
Forgot a while His power great,
Humbled Himself, took human form
And stripped Himself of royal state.

For Christ was also Man; to feel
Man's strongest tempting, and to know
His utmost weakness, He became
Like other men and suffered so.
And touched with our infirmities,
For those few years like us to be,
He still remembers we are dust,
Since He was tempted like as we.
But well He knew the source of help,

Whence comes all power, strength and peace,
In blest communion with His God, Care and perplexity
    would cease
When all earth's sorrow and its sin
Too heavy on His spirit weighed,
Quiet and solitude He sought
And to His Father prayed."

Annie Johnson Flint

Jesus told His disciples to pray (Matt. 26:41). He set an example which was ever before them. We read in Mark 1:35, 36 "And in the morning, rising up a great while before day, he went out, and departed into a solitary place and there prayed. And Simon and they that were with Him followed after him:" See also Mark 6:46.

He gave thanks. (Mark 14:23); He prayed alone, Matt. 14:23); He prayed in great earnestness. (Matt. 26:36-39); He prayed at His baptism (Luke 3:21).

(4) He was a man of obedience.

He made it plain that He came to do His Father's will. (Luke 22:42); (John 4:34); (John 6:40). He came in obedience to the Father to speak for Him (John 3:34).

(5) He was a man of sacrifice.

He became the lamb of Exodus 12:5, the lamb without blemish. "Forasmuch as ye know that ye were not redeemed with corruptible things, as silver and gold, from your vain conversation received by tradition from your fathers, but with the precious blood of Christ, as of a lamb without blemish and without spot: (I Peter 1:18, 19). Also see I Peter 3:18; John 1:29.

An illustration follows which was taken from "Illustrations of Bible Truth" by H. A. Ironside. "A friend of mine, himself an evangelist, lay for many weary months in a Roman Catholic hospital in the city of Oakland, California, because of injuries received in an automobile accident. On a nearby bed lay a young priest, evidently a sincere and earnest man, but he was greatly troubled in view of possible death. An aged priest came from time to time to hear his confessions, and to grant him absolution. My friend longed to speak to him, but found him very difficult to approach.

One day, however, as the older priest was about to leave, he overheard the young one say to him, something like this, "Father, it is very strange; I have done everything I know to do. I have sought to carry out all that the church has asked, and yet I have no peace. How can I be sure that God has put away my sins?"

The other looked at him compassionately, and then exclaimed, "Surely the blood of Christ ought to count for something!"

As though a flash of divine light had entered his soul, the young priest's countenance changed. He looked up eagerly to exclaim, "Ah, yes, it counts for everything. I can trust that." It was evident afterwards that his soul had entered into peace."

We would like to quote a passage from "The Person and Work of Christ" by Benjamin B. Warfield, page 571.

"Nevertheless, let us rejoice that our God has not left us by searching to find Him out. Let us rejoice that He has plainly revealed Himself to us in His Word as a God who loves us, and who, because He loves us, has sacrificed Himself for us. Let us remember that it is a fundamental conception in the Christian idea of God that God is love; and that it is the fundamental dogma of the Christian religion that God so loved us that He gave Himself for us. Accordingly, the primary presupposition of our present passage is that our God was capable of, and did actually perform, this amazing act of unselfish self-sacrifice for the good of man."

(5) He was a man of wisdom.

Even at twelve years of age Jesus astounded learned people of His day. See Luke 2:41-52. Again in the temple, Luke tells us in 4:22 , "And all bare Him witness, and wondered at the gracious words which proceeded out of His mouth. And they said, "Is not this Joseph's son?" Read the reaction to His wisdom in Mark 6:2, 3.

(6) He was a man who expressed His love.

That Jesus was a person of warmth and love we see clearly in His attitude toward children. That He gave them attention, blessed them and prayed for them astounded others. (Matt. 18:2; Matt. 19:13, 14). Sometimes we see unusual spiritual qualities in children. They trust, they adore, they have great faith. Jesus lovingly held them in His arms and no doubt enjoyed the response He received. But He also saw their great value.

Even as Jesus reached out to children, He held forth His hands to the laboring man and woman. One of His best known statements is found in Matt. 11:28, "come unto me, all ye that labour and are heavy laden, and I will give you rest." He expressed His love for the working world.

We gain from these verses two facts. (1) We have a God who can love and (2) we have a God who can feel.

(7) He was a man of no discrimination.

We see His attitude in His association with the woman at the well in John 4:9. She was no doubt surprised as Jesus approached because she was used to discrimination. He not only spoke to her but for the first time revealed that He was the Messiah. He never held Himself aloof. He loved women and defended them when they came under fire, see Mark 14:3-9. His lack of discrimination caused Him to be criticized (Luke 15:2). When He came in contact with Zacchaeus, or Mary Magdalene, or a rich young ruler Jesus never changed His attitude.

(8) He was a man of modesty.

Few leaders would say, "I am meek and lowly." It would ruin their image. In Matt. 11:29, 30 and Phil. 2:7, 8 we see a brief glimpse of the meek (but not weak) Saviour who came from heaven to accept the image of sinful flesh that man might be redeemed.

(9) He was a man who saw into the heart of man.

We see in John 13:21 one of the Lord's most troubled moments. He knew His betrayer, even though there had been no outward sign of the degenerate heart of Judas. Jesus experienced pain, sadness and loss as He perceived what was in the heart of Judas and sat with this disciple for the last time in fellowship.

Because He *saw* He exposed the evil works which are in the heart and which come forth to defile. Mark 7:21-23. His strongest words were directed at the pharisees who He said "Do all their works to be seen of men" Matt. 23:5. He was so stirred by what He saw as a religious covering that He denounced them with what is called the "seven woes." See Matt. 23:13-29.

He Was a Teacher Sent from God (John 12:49,50)

Jesus Christ, God's son referred to His teachings as "My Words" or "My Sayings." In the Greek these words are "Logos" and "Rhēma." There is some distinction of meaning but not of importance in these words. "Logos" primarily means a method of expression and truth which is expressed. "Rhēma" means articulate speech which conveys a meaning. For example in Matt. 7:24 we read, "Therefore, whosoever heareth *these sayings of mine,* and doeth them, I will liken him unto a wise man, which built his house upon a rock:" In Matt. 24:35 "Heaven and earth shall pass away, but *my words* shall not pass away." The important fact is that "my words" and "my sayings" were teachings that came from a teacher sent from God and which are the most important statements in our Bibles. "For I have not spoken of myself; but the Father which sent me, he gave me a commandment, what I should say, and what I should speak. And I know that His commandment is life everlasting: whatsoever I speak therefore, even as the Father said unto me, so I speak." John 12:49, 50. Jesus, Himself, put the insignia of His Father upon His words and His sayings.

In John 7 we have an interesting incident concerning Jesus. Officers had been sent by the chief priests and pharisees to arrest Jesus. When they came back without Him they were asked, "Why did you not bring Him?" Had He escaped from them? Did He resist arrest? Had they not been able to find Him? None of these problems were responsible for their empty hands. They had listened to Him as He taught and they either forgot what they had come for, or else decided on their own that such a teacher could not do wrong. They answered, "Never man spake like this man." John 7:46. They were stating the truth for no man ever taught like Jesus did. To consider Him as a teacher only, is a fatal mistake. But to consider His teaching as One who is God and who was a teacher sent from God opens to us the love of God in the fullest sense.

(1) Christ taught with absolute authority. Matt. 7:29.

As a teacher Christ was unique, outshining all earthly teachers as the sun outshines all candles. As a rule, the greater the teacher the more readily he will admit that his is not the last word, that there is room for further investigation and for questioning. But Jesus insisted that His word was final, that there was no other right way. For instance when He said, "But I say unto you" He assumed absolute and divine authority (carefully consider Matt. 5:21, 22; 27-28; 43-44).

When He said: "Verily, verily I say unto thee, except a man be born again, he cannot see the kingdom of God," (John 3:3), He left no room for a difference of opinion on the subject. We also notice that He taught with absolute authority on subjects that are mysteries to man, such questions as "Is there life after death? "Is there a real Hell?" "Is there a real Devil?" "Are angels a reality?" Jesus answered all these questions. He was never vague. He never used such subjunctive phrases as "I suppose," "Maybe," "I think," "Perhaps," In fact the subjunctive mood is completely absent from His teaching.

On the question of life after death he said: "I am the resurrection and the life. He that believeth in me, though he were dead, yet shall he live." John 11:25.

As to the reality of Heaven, He said: "In my Father's house are many mansions, if it were not so, I would have told you." John 14:2.

Regarding the reality of Hell, He stated, "Where the worm dieth not, and the fire is not quenched." Mark 9:44.

Is the Devil a real person or fiction? Jesus said: "I beheld Satan as lightening fall from heaven." Luke 10:18; Mark 8:33.

Concerning angels He reported: "And it came to pass that the beggar died and was carried by the angels into Abraham's bosom" Luke 16:22.

When questioned about man's chances to be right with God He answered, "Verily, verily I say unto thee, except a man be born again, he cannot see the kingdom of God." John 3:3.

Speaking on the reliability of the Scripture, He declared: "For verily I say unto you, Till heaven and earth pass, one jot or one tittle shall in no way pass from the law, till all be fulfilled." Matt. 5:18.

(2) Christ claimed that His teaching would last forever. He said in Matt. 24:35 "Heaven and earth shall pass away but my words shall not pass away."

It is a breath taking fact that His words have not passed away. Though it was said of Him, ". . . How knoweth this man letters, having never learned?" John 7:15. His teachings have stood every test of time and investigation. They have never been in error, become obsolete, or been improved upon. They are as up to date today as when they were first uttered in Palestine. When compared with the everchanging text books of man's learning, Christ's teaching stands alone as having never needed to be changed. His words have passed into a thousand languages, but they have not passed away.

(3) Christ's teaching is completely free from the superstitions of His time. Study John 9:1-4; Luke 13:1-5.

The world of Jesus' day was full of superstitions which played no small part in what people believed and in what they did. Even the disciples of Jesus were subject to some of the superstitions held by the people in general. But not so with the Lord Jesus. Not one superstition did He endorse. When faced with one, He quickly declared it to be invalid. The fact that He never endorsed a single superstition is one of the strong evidences of His divine origin. It gives meaning to His claim, "I am the truth." John 14:6.

(4) Christ presented Himself as the center of His teaching. It is impossible to separate Christ from His message, for He made Himself the center of His message. This fact is either another evidence of His Deity, or else it is evidence of unparalleled conceit. Compare the following scriptures which are samples of how He made himself the center of His teaching. John 5:39, 40; John 8:12; John 10:27-30; John 11:24, 25; John 14:1-6; John 15:4, 5.

(5) The great burden of Christ's teaching was the value of the soul above that of the body and the importance of being right with

God over everything else in a person's life. See Matt. 16:24-26.

His mind was forever occupied with man's need of being right with God. He never lost sight of this, and gave His life in order to make it possible. If we may speak of Jesus having an obsession, then it is His great endeavor to awaken people to their great need of being right with God. He would try to awaken them to this need by asking startling questions, such as "For what is a man profited, if he shall gain the whole world, and lose his own soul?"

He used such a shocking statement as "If the eye offend thee, pluck it out, it is better for thee to enter into the kingdom of God with one eye, than having two eyes to be cast into hell fire." Mark 9:47.

He used a variety of significant parables and stories, such as the Rich Man and Lazarus (Luke 16:19-30), and the Rich Fool (Luke 12:16-21).

He told of great gladness in Heaven over one sinner who turned to God (Luke 15:3-10), and pictured the God of Heaven as being in a hurry when one soul turns homeward to Him (Luke 15:20-24).

To His disciples Jesus declared that the greatest cause for rejoicing is a person's assurance that his name is included in Heaven's register (Luke 10:20), and that the kingdom of God and His righteousness is the most important matter in every person's life and should receive our first attention. (Matt. 6:33).

(6) He confirmed that the Old Testament Scriptures were true. Deuteronomy was a favorite book. He quoted the Ten Commandments except the eighth. He referred to the prophets. See Mark 10:19, also Matt. 10:39, 40, 41.

(7) He taught about love, giving us a new commandment. "And thou shalt love the Lord thy God with all thy heart, and with all thy soul, and with all thy mind, and with all thy strength: this is the first commandment. And the second is like, namely this, Thou shalt love thy neighbor as thyself. There is none other commandment greater than these." Mark 12:30, 31.

"A new commandment I give unto you, that ye love one another; as I have loved you, that ye also love one another. By this shall all men know that ye are my disciples, if ye have love one to another." Read John 13:34, 35.

"But I say unto you which hear, love your enemies, do good to them which hate you, bless them that curse you, and pray for them which despitefully use you." Luke 6:27-39.

(Note) The following five points concerning Christ's teachings are adapted from the splendid little book "Basic Christianity" by John R. Scott, page 26; published by William B. Eerdmans Publishing Company, Grand Rapids, Michigan.

1. Christ stated that to know Him was to know God. "If ye had known me, ye should have known my Father also (John 8:19). Also compare John 14:7.

2. Christ suggested that to see Him was to see God. "He that hath seen me, hath seen the Father" (John 14:9) "And he that seeth me seeth him that sent me" (John 12:45).

3. Christ implied that to believe in Him was to believe in God, and to refuse to believe in Him was to refuse to believe in God. "He that believeth on me, believeth not on me but on him that sent me" (John 12:44); (John 14:1).

4. Christ declared that to honor Him was to honor God and to reject honoring Him would be the same as refusing to honor God. "That all men should honor the Son, even as they honor the Father. He that honoreth not the Son, honoreth not the Father which hath sent Him." (John 5:23).

Note: These words are as plain and as strong as words can be, leaving no doubt whatever that Christ insisted that whatever treatment people accord Him, is also accorded God.

(5) Christ insisted that to hate Him was to hate God. "He that hateth me hateth my Father also." (John 15:23).

What Jesus Taught About His Own Death

"Not my will . . . thy will be done." Matt. 26:36-47. The rest of the Word of God agrees with this. Compare such verses as I Peter 1:18-20; Rev. 13:8; Isa. 53:10.

Jesus insisted that his sacrificial death was the real purpose of His coming into the world. See John 12: 23, 24; also John 12:27-33; Matt. 16:21-23.

Christ taught that His death on the cross was absolutely necessary for the salvation of man. See Luke 24: 6-8; Luke 24:25-27; Luke 24:44-46; Luke 17:23, 24, 25; Luke 9:21, 22; John 3:14-16.

What Jesus Taught About the Believer

In the book of John we find many teachings of Jesus concerning His believers. (1) He will behold His glory, John 17:24; (2) Christ is glorified in us, John 17:10; John 17:22 (3) We are honored by the Father, John 12:26; (4) We are judged by Jesus Christ, John 5:22; (5) We have everlasting life, being passed from death unto life, John 5:24; (6) We shall never perish, John 10:28; (7) we have a home in heaven, John 14:2; (8) We will be received when He comes again. John 14:3.

As we refer to the ministry of Jesus Christ we are using a term used by the Lord Himself. He said in Matt. 20:28 that "He came not to be ministered unto but to minister, and to give His life as a ransom for many." He came to present Himself as the Messiah by whom the kingdom of God was to be established. See John 4:26. These were His two great motives.

The great channels of His ministry were His miracles and His teaching. In His miracles He demonstrated His power as the Son of God; in His teaching He brought forth the words of God in simple, clear statements. In the miracles recorded we have only those which represent "kinds" of miracles. We have recorded the healing miracles; power over nature declared; exorcisms, or His power over Satanic influence; people being raised from the dead to demonstrate power over the enemy of death.

In His ministry, His path was clear and unchanging. A mere man would perhaps have been influenced by those who would have made him an earthly king, but Jesus Christ pursued a constant course from His birth in Bethlehem until at last He completed His mission on the cross of Calvary. John 19:30.

Questions for Consideration

(1) What can we learn from the ministry of Jesus Christ about God's love?

(2) What part of Christ's ministry was most amazing to the people of His day?

(3) Why are His words so important?

(4) What personal characteristic of Jesus is most unusual?

(5) What proofs do we find in Christ's ministry that He is God?

(6) Why did He give a new commandment?

(7) What did He teach about His death?

(8) What is His great promise to the Believer?

CHAPTER 11

The Love of God As Seen
In His Forgiveness

Suggested Reading: Psalm 32 and Luke 15:11-32

David said, "Blessed is he whose transgression is *forgiven,* whose sin is covered." Psalm 32:1. Forgiveness in the Bible means to lift the guilt from our backs and to carry it out of sight. We often speak of a "load of sin" or our "burden of sin." These are appropriate phrases because sin bows the heart and body. Forgiveness removes the load and the burden. In Luke 7:40-50 we find one of the best explanations of forgiveness. Jesus related the story of the two debtors, "There was a certain creditor which had two debtors: the one owed five hundred pence, and the other fifty. And when they had nothing to pay, he frankly forgave them both. Tell me therefore, which of them will love him most?" (Luke 7:41,42). The context shows that this meant the debt was removed, canceled, and the debtors owed nothing but gratitude.

It is the same with God's love as we see it in His forgiveness. The forgiven one has his debt of sin lifted, erased, blotted from the ledger. Examine Psalm 86:5, (God is good and ready to forgive); Psalm 103:3 (He forgives the vilest sin); God has power to forgive sin (Mark 2:10, Luke 5:24); Forgiveness is part of God's grace (Eph. 1:7).

God's Way of Forgiveness

God's only son came to "save His people from their sins" and He made the provision for complete forgiveness. In I John 2:2 we read, "And He is the propitiation (covering) for our sins: and not for ours only, but also for the sins of the whole world." Also see

Matt. 1:21; John 1:29; II Cor. 5:21. As the mercy seat in the Old Testament covered the broken law in the Ark of the Covenant, so the blood of Jesus Christ covers our sins from the sight of God. No other covering is adequate.

We are all familiar with barriers, especially those barricades we encounter on the highway. Even if there is a good reason behind a barricade—a bridge is out, a highway is dangerous or under construction—we still feel frustration when they appear before us. We are barred and the word is usually "detour." The word "forgiven" in the original text means "removed" or "taken away." When sin has erected a barrier between us and God, forgiveness removes that barrier. Fellowship with Him is restored and happiness follows. Man creates the barriers and it is God who stands ready to destroy them.

The Fact of Sin

The Bible stresses the actuality of sin and that it is God's will for us to rid ourselves of its presence in our lives (I John 1:9). We ourselves recognize evil and understand that it is a heartache to God. So it is important to know that God has provided a means of deliverance through the death of His Son, Jesus Christ. See Romans 3:25; Romans 5:8; Eph 4:32.

Getting back into the Old Testament we read in Lev. 17:11, "For the life of the flesh is in the blood; and I have given it to you upon the altar to make an atonement for your souls; for it is the blood that maketh an atonement for the soul."

Keep in mind that every blood sacrifice pointed to the substitutionary death of Christ.

Thousands of years before our scientists discovered the life giving properties of the blood in the human body and were ignorant of the life it carries as it courses through an intricate system of veins and arteries, the writer of Leviticus made a scientific statement "It is the blood which carries life."

Studying in the Congressional Library in Washington, D.C. I began reading about the terrible blood bath at Anzio, Italy, during the Second World War. Our troops were slaughtered and blood ran down the beach. It was a terrible catastrophe. The sacrifice of these men that day was made for freedom. My thoughts were serious as I meditated about the heroic effort. Once their blood had left their bodies they died. Life was gone. Leviticus was right, the life of the flesh is in the blood. Another thought came, the sacrifice was not in the blood contained in human bodies, it is in the blood which is shed, in this case loosed upon the sand of a beach. That beach became an altar for those men who died.

God, in His love planned our redemption and it was through His son that redemption is provided, "In whom we have redemption through His blood, the forgiveness of sins, according to the riches of His grace" Eph. 1:7. In redemption there is a price to be paid. But we know Jesus came as the "ransom-giver" the one who paid the price. The result of His sacrifice is that we have forgiveness of sins. (See Heb. 9:22). Understanding this we can have confidence that all sin has been taken care of through the Lord Jesus Christ.

There does exist a difference in the consciousness of sin. To those close to God, sin is much more disturbing. To those whose relationship is far from God, sin is accepted, glossed over and fails to stir the conscious. Even in the committing of a heinous crime we sometimes see no remorse.

(2) Sin left its mark on human nature.

From the time of Adam and Eve the human soul has been affected by sin. The mental part of man has not the command of thought or the purpose to keep it sin free. Sinful thoughts enter our minds easily (sometimes taking us by surprise). It is the mind, given as a blessing, which has produced some of the greatest destructive forces the world has ever known. It is the mental part of man which plans and schemes in the realm of immorality. God is truly a forgiving God to put up with our great offenses.

Emotionally we are sinful. Our rebellious natures persist in leading us astray. (Isa. 53:6). Our emotions of hate, malice, jealousy, distrust, bitterness, ingratitude, prejudice, unkindness, are ever present. We sympathize with Paul, the Apostle, as in Romans 7:15 he tells us, "For that which I do I understand not; for what I would that do I not; but what I hate, that do I." We see here an honest apostle, frustrated by mental and emotional problems. Much like as we are.

In spite of the marring work of sin, God sees in each person a soul, precious to Him because His own image is found here. We are marred but still loved. He sent His Son to provide a redemption which creates in us a new image, that of His son. Although still sinful, in our new relationship with God through Christ, the love of the darkness of sin may be counter-balanced by our love of God and our desire to glorify Him. II Peter 1:4.

God's Definite Statements

(1) Forgiveness of sin is through the sacrifice of Christ. (Heb. 9:26). Also see Heb. 9:12, 14, 22.

(2) It is no more called into remembrance. Jer. 31:34.

(3) It is cast into the depths of the sea. Micah 7:19.

(4) It is covered. Psalm 32:1, Deut. 33:12.

(5) It is blotted out. Psalm 51:9, Col. 2:14, Acts 3:19.

(6) Forgiveness brings a blessing. Psalm 32:1 This is a promise.

(3) To understand God's forgiveness we must see God as He really is.

Three words describe God: 1. omnipotent (unlimited power) 2. omnipresent (present in all places at all times) 3. omniscient (knowing all things). When we consider the meaning of these three words we shrink from descriptions of God as "the man upstairs" or "somebody up there." God as He really is has power with no limits, a presence which is everywhere and knowledge which includes all things.

We see He is *the God* of tender mercy (Psalm 51:1). It was not God's plan to condemn the world. Jesus stated God's purpose in John 3:17 "For God sent not his son into the world to condemn the world: but that the world through him might be saved. See Luke 15:7; I Tim. 1:15.

He feels compassion for the sinner and hears his voice (Psalm 55:16,17). In John 8:1-12 we have the incident of the woman taken in adultery. As we study this one event in the ministry of Jesus we see God's omnipotence, His omnipresence, His omniscience. But standing out is the great compassion Jesus had for this woman. ". . . Neither do I condemn thee; go and sin no more."

As the Son of God, Jesus demonstrated His power to forgive (Luke 5:24); He asserted that He forgave sinners (Luke 7:47); He gave instructions to His followers on forgiveness (Mark 11:25,26). See also II Cor. 2:7,10.

He Understands Our Temptations and Our Spiritual Battles

New believers are often bewildered when they discover that temptations are still with them. They expected to be free from lust, ugly thoughts and the impulses of the flesh. However, in Eph. 6:12 we read that the believer's life is a spiritual battleground—not a playground. It is a spiritual battleground as we struggle against principalities, powers, against the rulers of darkness of this world, against spiritual wickedness in high places. We are less than a match for these foes in our own strength than young David was against Goliath. But David did not come in his own strength. He said "I come to thee in the name of the Lord of hosts" (I Sam. 17:45).

We have a powerful enemy in Satan who works on us with his wiles (Eph. 6:11), but our battle need not be a losing one, for our Lord assures us, "Be of good cheer, I have overcome the world (John 16:33). Add to this the promise of the Holy Spirit, "Greater is he that is in you than he that is in the world" (Phil. 4:13), (I John 4:4). The central truth of Eph. 6:10-18 is that the whole power of Almighty God is at our disposal to meet our spiritual enemy, Satan, and we are able to stand up against all that he can throw at us, for we trust "In the power of *His* might." Eph. 6:10.

Thy Sins Are Forgiven Thee

"And behold, men brought in a bed a man which was taken with a palsy: and they sought means to bring him in, and to lay him before him. And when they could not find by what way they might bring him in because of the multitude, they went upon the house top, and let him down through the tiling with his couch into the midst before Jesus. And when he saw their faith, he said unto him, Man, thy sins are forgiven thee. And the scribes and the pharisees began to reason, saying, who is this which speaketh blasphemies? Who can forgive sins, but God alone? But Jesus perceived their thoughts, he answering said unto them, what reason ye in your hearts? Which is easier to say, Thy sins be forgiven thee; or to say, Rise up and walk? But that ye may know that the Son of Man hath authority upon earth to forgive sins (he said unto the sick of the palsy), I say unto thee, Arise, and take up thy couch, and go into thine house. And immediately he rose up before them, and took up that whereon he lay, and departed to his own house, glorifying God. And they were all amazed, and they glorified God, and were filled with fear, saying, we have seen strange things today."

Luke 5:18-26, Mark 2:1-13 relates the same incident in the ministry of Jesus.

Most religions recognize the problem of sin in the life and deal with it in different ways. There is the monk who seeks to withdraw from the world, believing it to be the inherent problem. Jesus prayed for His disciples but not that they be removed from the world and its influence, "I pray not that thou shouldst take them out of the world, but that thou shouldst keep them from the evil" (John 17:15).

There is the religion which thinks the body itself is the source of sin and tries to punish sin out by starvation, beating, or denying it any joy. There is religion that uses the mind to "think" out sin and bring the soul into a perfect relationship with the Creator. There is also religion which claims there is no sin.

With simplicity the Bible teaches us that sin and defilement are of spiritual and moral natures and come from an unclean heart (Jer. 17:9). We tend to view sin as we see it externally but God sees the internal source.

The palsied man in Luke 5 evidently had a strong consciousness of his sin. Jesus addressed Himself to this need first. He had great faith. He was helpless physically and spiritually. In this incident we see many interesting details. Jesus was teaching, a large crowd had gathered. Among those present were professional interpreters of the Mosaic law from Galilee and no doubt, Jerusalem. As Jesus taught and they listened men approached with a palsied friend, bringing him to Jesus that he might be healed. Finding no way to break through the crowd, they ascended (probably by an out-side stairway) to the roof of this house and then proceeded to make a hole in the roof so that they could lower the man into the room where Jesus taught.

If you have been to Palestine you know that these roofs are strong and heavy. It must have taken great effort to break through the tiles and make an opening large enough to let down a man on a pallet. It is evidence of the faith of all five that they had made the initial decision and then persisted under the circumstances. We can sense the amazement of those below as this took place.

Although this was early in the ministry of Jesus He had already established Himself as a teacher. Who would feel greater hostility than the other "teachers" who were gathered to hear Him? Jesus, however, gave His attention to the paralized man before Him. In one brief moment He understood the faith and desire of this man's heart. He spoke and His words caused consternation in the minds of the scribes and pharisees. He said, "Man, thy sins are forgiven thee."

Here we find the omniscience of Christ, dealing with the palsied man and also understanding the thoughts of the scribes and pharisees. This should have impressed the pharisees but they immediately began to criticize. They assumed that this was a mere man and even though he was a recognized healer, in forgiving sin He had invaded forbidden territory. They thought He was blaspheming God who from their teachings was the only one who could forgive sin.

Jesus asked a simple question: "Is it easier to say, Thy sins be forgiven thee or to say, Rise up and walk?" A miraculous healing is something visible and impressive. The forgiveness of sin is harder, because the scribes and pharisees were right, only God can forgive sin. Jesus spoke these very important words, "But that ye may know that the Son of Man hath power upon earth to forgive sins, (He said unto the sick of the palsy) I say unto thee, Arise, and take up thy couch, and go into thine house." This miracle was performed to substantiate His power to forgive sin. And He spoke with authority. This was something new—Christ proclaiming that sin could be forgiven by Him on earth. See Mark 2:17.

The Woman with the Alabaster Box

"And, behold, a woman in the city, which was a sinner, when she knew that Jesus sat at meat in the pharisee's house, brought an alabaster box of ointment, and stood at his feet behind him weeping, and began to wash his feet with tears, and did wipe them with the hairs of her head, and kissed his feet, and anointed them with the ointment.

Now when the pharisee which had bidden him saw it, he spake within himself, saying, This man, if he were a prophet, would have known who and what manner of woman this is that toucheth him, for she is a sinner. And Jesus answering said unto him, Simon, I have somewhat to say unto thee. And he saith, Master, say on. There was a certain creditor which had two debtors: the one owed five hundred pence, and the other fifty. And when they had nothing to pay, he frankly forgave them both. Tell me therefore, which of them will love him most? Simon answered and said, I suppose that he, to whom he forgave most. And he said unto him, Thou hast rightly judged. And he turned to the woman, and said unto Simon, seest thou this woman? I entered into thine house, and thou gavest me no water for my feet: but she hath washed my feet with tears, and wiped them with the hairs of her head. Thou gavest me no kiss: but this woman since the time I came in hath not ceased to kiss my feet. My head with oil thou didst not anoint: but this woman hath anointed my feet with ointment. Wherefore I say unto thee, her sins, which are many are forgiven; for she loved much: but to whom little is forgiven, the same loveth little. And he said unto her, Thy sins are forgiven. And they that sat at meat with him began to say within themselves, who is this that forgiveth sins also? And he said to the woman, Thy faith hath saved thee; go in peace." Luke 7:37-50

In this incident in the ministry of Jesus we have a wonderful disclosure of Christ dealing with a woman and forgiving her sins.

This woman was known to be a sinful person. Jesus did not deny her guilt or cover it up. She must have been a woman of courage because she knew when she came into the pharisee's house he would not be pleased. Although himself a sinner, he had labeled this woman as one of the worst sinners and wanted nothing to do with her. When she touched Jesus and He did not object, he began to have doubts about Jesus. The tears and the kissing of His feet meant nothing to the pharisee.

"Jesus said to Simon, "Seest thou this woman?" The pharisee saw what we might call a "disgrace to the community." Jesus saw much more. He did not refer to her sin or reputation, but He spoke of her spiritual sensitivity to Himself and her worshipful attitude. One woman, two different views.

Jesus spoke only a few words to the woman, "Thy sins are forgiven, Thy faith hath saved thee, go in peace." We should compare John 8:1-11 where Jesus dealt with another sinful woman. In both cases faith had reached into the heart.

Jesus was fully representing His Father. See Jer. 31:34. He gave forgiveness to the woman with the alabaster box and her fear of eternal judgment was removed. She now faced the world with a new relationship and the peace which had eluded her.

The attitude of the pharisee is still with us. A Christian friend of mine told me, "I did something today of which I am ashamed." He went on to say that as he drove into town, he passed a woman walking in the rain. His first inclination was to give her a ride and then as he drew closer and saw who it was he thought, "she has a bad reputation." So he drove on. Afterwards he felt shame which brought tears to his eyes as he talked. The Lord was showing him something about himself.

The pharisee had no feelings of compassion for the woman who was interrupting his dinner. He clearly thought she had no business to be there. There were others present but it was to this woman that Jesus gave forgiveness. Psalm 34:18 tells us, "The Lord is near unto those who are of a broken heart and saveth such as be of a contrite spirit." See Isa. 43:25.

When Jesus described the forgiveness of God He told the story of the prodigal son. The Scripture in Luke 15:11-32 should be read. In verse 20 we read, "When he was yet a long way off, his father saw him." We have the impression from this verse that the father had been anxiously waiting.

God has perfect remembrance. (Hosea 7:2) He knew every detail of his sons dissolute life, his arrogant spirit, his final confession of sin and his desire to return to the father. But as this father saw his son coming from a long way off, compassion and love prompted him to run and embracing him, he kissed him. The father saw the dirt, the hunger, the damaged ego, the sorrow about sin. These he ignored, because the son was already forgiven.

For the returning son's filthy clothes, his father gave him a covering of the best robe in the house, then he added a ring. For the tired, bruised feet he found new shoes. For the famished body he had a fat calf killed. For a broken spirit, he offered the joy of a celebration. Here we see what Jesus wanted us to see, God receiving a broken life and with love and tenderness restoring it to His fellowship. How well Jesus used a simple story to illustrate God's forgiveness.

David Writes of God's Forgiveness

In Romans 4:6,7,8, Paul writes, "Even as David also describeth the blessedness of the man unto whom God imputeth righteousness apart from works, saying Blessed are they whose iniquities are forgiven and whose sins are covered. Blessed is the man to whom the Lord will not impute sin." Paul refers to the 32nd Psalm written by David after he had committed a terrible sin and was forgiven by the Lord.

In I Samuel we read much of the detailed life of David. Several points are interesting: (1) He had a good home and grew up to be a handsome youth with great potential and talent. (2) He was anointed by Samuel after a definite choosing by the Lord (I Sam. 16:13). The spirit of the Lord came upon David. (3) He had many experiences in which the Lord stood by him (I Sam. 17:45); (I Sam. 19:10); (I Sam. 24:4). (4) He was a man of pity and compassion (I Sam. 24:10), a man after God's own heart.

David's relationship with the Lord was truly wonderful and yet this man sinned a dreadful sin. His harp was stilled by sin. The writer of the wonders of God had nothing to sing about. Instead, an overwhelming uproar filled his soul. It was after David confessed his sin and received forgiveness that he wrote Psalm 32.

This Psalm is an intimate disclosure of the suffering that comes when a Believer falls into sin. Psalm 32 also reveals to us God's love in His pardoning grace.

We give this brief outline.
1. Happy is the man whose sin is forgiven. (verse 1)
2. Broken fellowship with God produces misery. (verse 3,4)
3. Confession brings forgiveness. (verse 5)
4. Conviction is miserable. (verse 10)
5. David was specific about his sin. (verse 5)

6. Believers are encouraged to seek the Lord for forgiveness. (verse 10)
7. New joy came to David after forgiveness. (verses 7,10,11)
8. We are admonished to be joyful that God forgives. (verse 11)

It is told of Luther that one day being asked which of the Psalms were the best, he made answer, "Psalmi Paulini," and when his friends pressed to know which these might be he said, "The 32nd, the 51st, and the 130th, and the 143rd. For they all teach that the forgiveness of our sins comes, without the law and without works, to the man who believes, and therefore I call them Pauline Psalms." From Luther's Table Talk (Treasury of David by C.H. Spurgeon, volume 2, page 86).

We learn some lessons from this experience of David. First, that even a good relationship with God can be broken; second, God having forgiven sin gives joy; third, forgiveness is an evidence of His love.

"I, even I, am he who blotteth out thy transgressions for my own sake, and will not remember thy sins." Isa. 43:25.

The Example of God the Father and His Son

All through the Old and New Testaments, we find God showing His love through forgiveness. When we think that God foreknew the death of His Son and that it would be cruel and humiliating, we see the strength of His love. He knew about the scourging, the mocking, the casting of dice for the apparel of His Son. And yet God, in His Son, could pray that these cruel representatives of the human race would be forgiven. This is love which has passed the highest test.

The Lord Jesus Christ demonstrated for us His forgiveness. The cross which He was made to carry, the nails which left prints in His hands show us the wonder of His forgiveness. At Calvary, He faced bitter foes who were determined to put Him to death. And yet, it was His own voice which uttered these words, "Father, forgive them, for they know not what they do." Luke 23:34. In that desperate hour Jesus proved that He and His Father were truly one in forgiveness.

In summing up God's love as seen in His forgiveness we notice some important facts.
(1) God seeks the sinner. See Gen. 3:9; Luke 19:10.
(2) It is God's desire to reshape the marred life. Jer. 18:1-4; John 15:2.
(3) There is no rebuke from God when He forgives. Luke 7:50.

(4) God, in Christ, reconciled the world unto Himself, forgiving sin. II Cor. 5:19.

(5) The greatest blessing is forgiveness and a life of fellowship with the Father. Psalm 128:1, 2.

God's Love and the Problem of Temptation

Temptation is not a sin. The Lord Jesus Christ was tempted. See Matt. 4:1-11. Temptation is seen in the Garden of Eden and has been with us ever since. It's serious consequence is that it may lead us to commit sin.

The sinister being behind temptation is Satan. It is his sole objective to induce the Believer to act from and for ourselves, independent of or in direct rebellion against God. His motive is to destroy our fellowship with God and to smudge the image we bear of Christ. To accomplish this he uses trickery, deceit, beguilement and all manner of stratagems fitting to the occasion. His methods are permeated with slyness.

Satan has a great variety of forms of temptation. In his cleverness, he suits his temptations to the individual, seeking out the weak spot in the personality. He is a foe to be reckoned with.

Consider how cleverly he worked on Peter, the brash young disciple who declared, "Though I should die with thee, yet will I not deny thee . . ." (Matt. 26:35). What a joy must have filled Satan when Peter denied knowing the Lord. See Matt. 26:69-75.

Notice that Peter had already left the Lord (Matt. 26:56) and now apparently he had come quietly back to be near Him.

We find these statements: He sat by the enemy's fire to enjoy its warmth (Luke 22:55); He completely lost his integrity before the sharp eyes of a young girl (Mark 14:67); He cursed to protect himself (Mark 1:71); He persisted in a lie.

The best part of the incident is found in Mark 14:72. Peter wept as he remembered Jesus' words, "Before the cock crows twice, thou shalt deny me thrice." He wept as his yielding to temptation became clear. In Luke 22:61 there is a simple statement, "And the Lord turned and looked upon Peter." The compassion and understanding of the "look" pierced his heart. The temptation was so great that Peter fell without a struggle. He loved Jesus but before Satan's onslaught his spiritual defense crumpled.

Not all temptations are so great or so dramatic. There are all the temptations which lead into the commission of sin and others which are temptations to not do that which we ought.

Since we cannot eliminate temptation, Eph. 6 gives us some instructions about dealing with this problem.

1. We pray (Eph. 6:18).
2. We have faith (Eph. 6:16).
3. We use the sword of the Word. (Eph. 6:17). Since Jesus in His great temptation used the Word, it is important to realize its value in dealing with temptation. Loving the Word of God and knowing it is a great restraint against giving in to temptation. The Word of God cleanses and purifies a corrupt nature. It acts as a frame to the Christian life and the end result is a life that is pure on the inside and the outside. It illuminates the daily walk, where temptation lies waiting.

Love is the bond which knits these three truths together and which produces an effective armor against temptation.

We find it is God's love, "There hath no temptation taken you but such as is common to man: but God is faithful, who will not suffer you to be tempted above that ye are able; but will with the temptation also make a way to escape, that ye may be able to bear it." I Cor. 10:13. Also see Prov. 8:17; Heb. 2:18; Hosea 14:4.

We find it is our love, "I will love thee, O Lord, *my strength.*" Psalm 18:1. Also see Matt. 10:37, Rev. 2:4.

Questions to be Considered

1. Who has made provision for the forgiveness of sin?
2. What was the significance of the blood sacrifice in the Old Testament?
3. What happens to forgiven sin?
4. How can we fight against the onslaught of Satan?
5. What are the characteristics of God's forgiving nature?
6. When does temptation become sin?

CHAPTER 12

The Love of God As Seen
In His Greatness

Suggested Reading: Psalm 19; Psalm 37

"For great is our Lord, and of great power; his understanding is infinite," (Psalm 147:5).

In this chapter concerning the love of God, we say in exultation with Daniel, "Blessed be the name of God for ever and ever; for wisdom and might are His" Dan. 2:20. When we consider, even briefly, the greatness of the God who made us and who loves us, we find it difficult to express all the deep feeling of our grateful hearts. With David in Psalm 47 we exclaim "We praise Him!" We praise Him for His *great* Salvation; we praise Him in song and inner thoughts; we praise Him as we pray, remembering His concern; we praise Him for His patience and daily provision. And we know that He deserves much more praise than we give Him.

Especially we praise and thank Him for the Bible which tells us what God is really like. An unknown God cannot be fully trusted, served or worshipped. Our intelligent worship of God is in direct proportion to our knowledge and appreciation of Him. Someone once said, "To know Him is to love Him, and to love Him is to know Him." To know Him is to realize that He is indeed "a great God."

God Is Great in Wisdom

There is a difference made in the Bible between knowledge and wisdom. In I Cor. 12:8 where Paul speaks of the exercise of spiritual gifts he distinguishes between the word of wisdom and the word of knowledge. To have knowledge is to know facts; to have wisdom means to know how to use the knowledge about the facts. When applying these things to our own experience, we might say that almost anybody can secure knowledge simply by studying about a certain subject and by learning all the facts. Wisdom requires much more.

For an example, a man might know all the facts about the law of motion and learn all there is to be learned about the mechanical make-up of an automobile and still not have enough wisdom to slow down for a curve. At any university there are offered enough courses of study to keep a man studying for 100 years, 10 hours a day. Yet a man might take as many courses as possible and still not have enough wisdom to earn a living.

When we speak of the wisdom of God we find that the Bible tells us that God is perfect in wisdom. It speaks of the riches of His wisdom, and in fact He is called in the Bible "the only wise God" meaning that there is simply no comparison and that He stands alone when it comes to wisdom.

We find that God is wise in acting to a right end. He chooses the right way and pursues it until that work is accomplished. There is no random planning in God's affairs. God sticks to the wisest course and the end of all His works is perfect. He works all things according to the counsel of His own will (Eph. 1:11). The wisdom of God is God acting righteously, in justice, in absolute truth and in power. He can no more act unwisely than He can act in untruth.

Wisdom is an attribute of God and we find it linked to His knowledge (Rom. 11:33). His wisdom is eternal, just as he is eternal. Paul exclaims, "O the depth of the riches both of the wisdom and knowledge of God! How unsearchable are his judgments, and his ways past finding out!" Romans 11:33.

God's Wisdom in Creation and Operation of the Universe

"The Lord by wisdom hath founded the earth; by understanding He established the heavens." Proverbs 3:19,20.

Jeremiah also tells us "He hath made the earth by His power, He hath established the world by His wisdom, and hath stretched out the heavens by His discretion." Jer. 10:12.

Some years ago a few of us planned to build a new church. We engaged an architect and told him what we wanted. Finally the new church was completed and we moved in. During the next eight years we gradually came face to face with the awful mistakes which we had made. The vestibule proved to be much too small and became a real bottleneck. We had forgotten to provide for a nursery and the one we finally built in as an afterthought was much too small. The kitchen was so small and impracticable as to be almost unusable. The wall construction was the worst mistake, for the water leaked through it with every rain and that problem was never solved in spite of about a dozen water proofings. We are faced with the fact that in spite of considerable building experience, we just did not have the wisdom to plan for the very best results. We finally spent $100,000 in rebuilding the front end and we determined not to make the same mistakes—but we made a few new ones. Now we have some leaks which mystify us completely.

But God created a universe with countless suns and planets. He founded this earth and planned for its continued inhabitancy by man. As we look at it today, we can only bow our heads in reverance and admit that He thought of everything.

In Job 28:20-27 we read "Whence cometh wisdom? and where is the place of understanding? Seeing it is hid from the eyes of all living, and kept close from the fowls of the air. Destruction and death say, We have heard the fame hereof with our ears. God understandeth the way thereof. For He looketh to the ends of the earth, and seeth under the whole heaven; and He weigheth the waters by measure. When He made a decree for the rain, and way for the lightning of the thunder: then did He see it, and declare it; He prepared it, yea, and searched it out."

In these verses we are told that in His wisdom God planned for the watering of the earth through rain from the clouds. In planning this, God weighed the wind and the water (verse 25,26).

The first part of God's creation of the firmament was directed toward the establishing of the atmosphere. Even as light is necessary to life, water is necessary and God wisely made this provision for all living creatures. According to Genesis 1:6, the purpose of the atmosphere was to "divide the waters from the waters." This wonderful act of God made possible nature's watering system for the earth. By placing the atmosphere around the earth, God produced an unspeakably marvelous system by which the earth could receive water. Some of the water was to be in the sky (who but God would have thought of this?) in the form of clouds and vapor. The big oceans, lakes, rivers and seas were to be below, covering three-fourths of the earth's surface. More exciting than our great bodies of water is the ocean above our heads, suspended in vapor form and obedient to the will of God.

When the temperature drops in God's upper ocean, the vapor condenses into crystals and comes down to earth as rain, hail, snow, dew or fog. In verse 13 of Psalm 104, David says, "He watereth the hills from his chambers." An exact translation would read, "He watereth the hills from His upper rooms." And then God skillfully takes that same water from His lower ocean back into the atmosphere and converts it into showers. Scientifically we say, the sun shines upon the ocean causing the ocean's surface water to vaporize. In this process all the salt and other minerals are removed and pure water rises into the atmosphere or into God's "upper rooms."

We have a great God! He weighed the winds and He weighed the waters when He made a decree for the rain. He knew how to solve the problem of watering the earth. With God nothing is impossible! Psalm 104:13.

In Job 38:4-7 we find God speaking of the fixing of the world in space. There was great power and wisdom in this act of God. It took a divine Creator to place so large a body in its orbit so that never would it encounter any kind of collision or jar. When the task was finished, this planet of our existence was so well engineered that its motion may continue forever. It moves silently and perfectly and only in recent ages has man realized that it moved at all. Job said, "God hangeth the earth upon nothing." Indeed, God hanged the earth upon nothing, and it hangs very well. Its foundations are absolutely sure.

God has given us an earth full of riches and sea filled with treasure. The miracles of the earth are apparent but also we find the miracles of the sea a credit to the wisdom of an Almighty God. Think of the innummerable forms of life in the sea! The number and variety of species is far greater than that on land. Life in microscopic form is so plentiful that each drop of sea water is a world in itself.

Then there is the miracle of the great ocean currents which make sections of the north inhabitable to man. Ocean currents are wide streams of water, such as the Gulf stream, which move with terrific force in certain patterns, apparently carried onward by the Trade Winds and the rotation of the earth. The Gulf Stream is a huge mass of water which moves in a steady flow and in a fixed pattern toward the north and east. When it comes out of the Gulf of Mexico its warm waters move toward Europe, warming the air and making the whole northern part of Europe habitable for man. Consider the fact that Rome, in southern Italy, is actually situated north of New York City. Far to the north lie the countries of England, Scotland, Sweden, Norway, Finland, Denmark, Poland and Germany. All of these would be frozen areas without the warm air created by the waters of the Gulf Stream. We see much of the Lord's wisdom in the great, wide sea.

According to the record in Genesis, God "made" the sun, moon and stars on the fourth day. It is of importance that we take special notice of the word "made" which in the Hebrew is the word "Asah." It stands in contrast to the Hebrew word "Borah" which is translated "created." The word "created" is used in three different verses in the first chapter of Genesis. We find it in verses 1, 21 and 27. To create means to bring into existence something out of nothing by the simple use of power. It is used each time where we are told that God brought into existence something new which had not existed in any form, namely, the creation of the universe, (Genesis 1:10), the creation of life, (Genesis 1:21), and the creation of man with spiritual life (Genesis 1:27).

The word "Asah" translated "made" in Genesis one, means to arrange, to organize into the desired form, as for example when man takes wool and organizes or makes it into a fine suit. We understand that the sun, moon and stars were already created in the original creation, but on the fourth day God arranged or organized them into the desired system to perform His purpose regarding the earth. The purpose of these heavenly bodies is to give light, heat, day and night, and the seasons and the years. The heavens display the glory of God and also His great wisdom.

A Practical Application to the Study of God's Wisdom

"The fear of the Lord is the beginning of wisdom" (Psalm 111:10). To "fear" the Lord is an Old Testament word or phrase which has nothing to do with being afraid of Him, but refers to the right attitude of man toward God in respecting, worshipping, trusting and obeying Him. The "fear" is the *beginning* of wisdom. Therefore, no person is living sensibly until he has taken God into account in his life and in his plans. See Job 28:28. Also Luke 12:16-21.

God's wisdom encourages us to trust Him. Since He has made no mistakes in planning the universe, we ought to be able to trust Him with our plans and with our problems.

God Is Great in His Power

The power of God is mentioned over 300 times in the Bible. By "the power of God" we understand that God has unlimited ability and strength to accomplish perfectly everything that He desires to do. This does not mean necessarily that God always does everything that He can do, for His power is always regulated by His wisdom and by His will. "Remember the former things of old: for I am God, and there is none like me. Declaring the end from the beginning, and from ancient times the things that are not yet done, saying, *My counsel shall stand, and I will do all my pleasure."* Isaiah 46:9, 10. Also see Psalm 115:3.

The study of the power of God is one of the most profitable studies in the Bible and will lead the believer to greater trust and praise of the God who redeemed us.

Biblical Expressions of the Greatness of God's Power

1. God's power is spoken of as His eternal power.

"For the invisible things of him from the creation of the world are clearly seen, being understood by the things that are made, even *his eternal power* and Godhead; so that they are without excuse." Romans 1:20. This means that God has always been almighty in His power and in His strength. He has not increased or grown in His ability, nor has His power decreased through the centuries.

2. The Bible speaks of the *exceeding greatness* of God's power.

"And what is the exceeding greatness of his power to us-ward who believe, according to the working of his mighty power." Eph. 1:19.

This verse describes the power which God has excercised in providing salvation for us, a power which broke all records in the use of his power.

3. The Bible states that God is *strong in power.*

"Lift up your eyes on high, and behold who hath created these things, that bringeth out their host by number: He calleth them all by names by the greatness of his might, for that he is *strong in power;* not one faileth." Isaiah 40:26.

So great is God's ability and so strong is His power that all of His creations in the universe function properly. In His creative power God gave His creations their present estate. It is His power which keeps them. Should God's power cease, all things would cease to be. This is especially true of the Christian of whom we read in Acts 17:28, "For in him we live, and move, and have our being; as certain also of your own poets have said, For we are also his offspring." As we were elevated to our present estate from being nothing, it is by His power that we remain.

4. Jesus taught that *with God all things are possible.*

"But Jesus beheld them, and said unto them, with men this is impossible; but with God all things are possible." Matt. 19:26.

This statement of Christ refers particularly to the grace of God which is able to save sinful man, even a rich man. However, it has a much wider application, meaning that nothing is impossible with God as far as His power to perform it is concerned. This fact will be seen in the next point.

5. The Bible declares that *nothing is too hard for God to do.*

"Ah Lord God! Behold, thou hast made the heaven and the earth by thy great power and stretched out arm, and there is nothing too hard for thee." Jer. 32:17.

The teaching of this chapter has to do with God's chastisement of Israel and His promises of finally restoring that people and making an everlasting covenant with them. There is nothing too hard for God, not even the bringing of Israel to conversion at the return of Jesus Christ.

"It is a comfort that power is in the hand of God; it can never be better placed, for he can never use His power to injure his confiding creature. If it were in our hands, we might use it to injure ourselves. It is a power in the hand of an indulgent father, not a hard-hearted tyrant; it is a just power. 'His right hand is full of righteousness' Psalm 48:10; because of His righteousness He can never use it ill, and because of his wisdom he can never use it unseasonably. Men that have strength often misplace the power of it, because of their folly, and sometimes employ it to base ends, because of their wickedness. But this power of God is always awakened by goodness and conducted by wisdom; it is never exercised by self-will and passion, but according to the immutable rule of his own nature, which is righteousness. How comfortable is it to think that you have a God that can do as he pleases; nothing so difficult but he can effect, nothing so strong but he can overrule! . . . For whom should that eternal arm of the Lord be displayed, and that imcomprehensible thunder of his power be shot out, but for those for whose sake and for whose comfort it is revealed in his words?" (Excerpt from The Existence and Attributes of God by Stephen Charnock, page 437.)

The Manifestations of God's Power

The power of God cannot be measured by man, but we do have some very excellent demonstrations of it.

1. God's power is demonstrated in the creation of the universe.

"For the invisible things of him from the creation of the world are clearly seen, being understood by the things that are made, even his eternal power and Godhead; so that they are without excuse." Romans 1:20, also see Psalm 150:1 and Psalm 19:1.

In Genesis 1:1 we are told that God created the universe. The

Hebrew word "Bara" which is used for "create" means to bring into existence out of nothing except as it comes out of God's own power, that is, out of the energy that is within Himself. This is something altogether foreign to the experience of man. All the united forces of nature, plus man helping, cannot produce anything out of nothing. With nature's help man may multiply and increase some things. He may also change some things from one form into another, like iron ore which is changed into a razor blade. But man cannot create or make something out of nothing. Yet God created the universe without matter, without advice, without instruments and without any help. See Isaiah 44:24 and Isaiah 40:12-14.

The recent explorations of man in space have given us a much better appreciation of the greatness of God's creation. In order to better understand the magnitude of the universe, let us consider the following. Suppose we would place in a room a big globe the size of a large tractor tire. This represents the sun. Then 600 yards away we will place a baseball and let that represent our earth. Six feet from the baseball we will place a very small marble, about the size of a pea which represents the moon. This arrangement will give us a fair idea of the proportion of distance and size within our solar system. If we can now imagine the whole United States covered with similar globes and balls and marbles of various sizes and distances, all of them moving and circling, then we will begin to get an idea of the greatness and complexity of the universe. All of this God created out of His great power. Yet, according to Psalm 33:6-9 He did not really exert Himself, "For he spake and it was done; he commanded and it stood fast."

At this point it is well for us to remember that it is this same God who loved us so that He "spared not His own Son but delivered Him up for us all." Romans 8:32.

2. God's power is demonstrated in His Son through whom He works. Jesus stated, "My Father worketh hitherto, *and I work.*" God's mighty power is found in the mighty power of His Son. "Who being the brightness of his glory, and the express image of his person, and upholding all things by the *word of his power. . .*" Hebrews 1:3. Col. 1:17 tells us" "And he is before all things, and by him all things consist."

As One with the Father the Son was also the wise and powerful creator for we read in Col. 1:16 "For by him were all things created that are in heaven, and that are in earth, visible and invisible, whether they be thrones, or dominions, or principalities, or powers: all things were created by him, and for him."

The law of physics says that there cannot be continuous action without the application of an external power. This is true in our experience, whether we consider the human body, which must eat to replenish the energy expended, or a watch or an automobile. What then keeps this universe functioning? The answer of the Bible is that God's might and power is applied to make it work.

3. God's power is demonstrated in His great plan of Salvation for man.

Eph. 1:17-20 should be studied as these verses contain a summary of what God has accomplished for man through the death and resurrection of Jesus Christ. This includes the "hope of our calling" and the "riches of the glory of his inheritance." All that is included in our salvation is the result of "the exceeding greatness of his power. . .which he wrought in Christ." verses 19, 20.

The words, "the exceeding greatness of his power" convey the idea in the original that this was the greatest use God ever made of His power. It took more to save man than to create the world with man in it.

This may seem incredible at first, but we can well believe it when we consider the following facts involved:

a. Our salvation involved the virgin birth of Jesus Christ. Through this birth God solved the problem of God becoming fully man without receiving a sinful nature. Though in Christ there was a union of both the nature of God and the nature of man, yet He was "without sin."

b. Our salvation involved the sacrificial death and subsequent resurrection of the God-Man, Christ Jesus. We must remember that God cannot die. Yet God the Son did die. God solved the problem.

c. Our salvation involved the problem of man's sinful nature which is opposed to God, or as the Bible states "is enmity against God" and "cannot please God." Romans 8:8, 9.

d. Our salvation involved the total opposition and defeat of Satan. In creation there was no one to oppose God.

e. Our salvation involved the holy law of God which had to be satisfied.

f. Our salvation involved the fact of death, which had to be overcome for man.

When all these factors are carefully considered, we may well understand that the reconciliation of sinful man to Himself via Bethlehem and Calvary was the greatest thing that God ever did. In the light of this, we will have a new appreciation of the statement in I Cor. 24 that "Christ is the power of God and the wisdom of God."

Hebrews 2:3 asks, "How shall we escape if we neglect so great a salvation?"

Contrasts Between God's Power and Man's Power

Is there anything that God can do which man cannot eventually do? The following contrasts will bring us down to earth:

1. Man needs matter to work upon and to work with. God does not need matter for He can create, make something out of nothing. There was a time when there was nothing but God.

2. Man needs hands and instruments to work with. God needs no hands nor instruments. "The worlds were framed by the word of God." Heb. 11:3.

3. Man needs a copy to work by. God works without copies and it is His works which furnish man with copies.

4. Man needs time in which to accomplish his work. God needs no time at all, for "He spake and it was done."

5. All that man makes depends upon an outside source of power for its operation. What God makes operates without any outside power.

For example, the worlds of the universe keep going in perpetual motion. The sun keeps sending forth its heat and light in undimmed power. The sea keeps producing life in a million varieties and sustains it perpetually. But man has never solved the secret of perpetual motion. Motors need fuel, light needs fuel, whether it be tallow or electricity.

6. Man's power is temporary and needs recuperation. God's power is continuous. He is never weary. See Isaiah 40:28.

7. Man cannot give life. God made man of the dust of the ground and breathed into his nostrils the breath of life and man became a living soul.

8. God's creations never fail. Man's works constantly need repair and replacement. See Isaiah 40:26.

Our Great God Is Unchangeable!

"There is no variableness nor shadow of turning with Him." James 1:17.

While all else changes God is unchangeable in all His attributes. His wisdom, His power and His will for mankind remains the same forever. It is His immutability which unites every attribute—if in any attribute He should fail He would no longer be the perfect God we can trust.

In finding a word to express this characteristic of God the Old Testament writers used the word "rock." See Deut. 32:4. We consider rock to signify firmness, strength, lasting qualities and something it is safe to build upon. Also see I Sam. 2:2 and Psalm 18:2.

Hebrews 13:8 is a great conclusion concerning the immutability of God. "Jesus Christ, the same yesterday, and today, and forever. For God the Father, God the Son and God the Holy Spirit, our Triune God, is indeed the same forever. In Daniel 6:26 we read, ". . .for he is the living God, and steadfast forever, and his kingdom that which shall not be destroyed, and his dominion shall be even unto the end." True words from King Darius. Time does not change our great God and circumstances do not alter His perfect will and wisdom. He alone is dependent upon no one.

Our prayers testify of our confidence in an unchanging Triune God. We do not expect God to change His relationship with us as His children. It is a "forever" relationship. We expect His love to be exactly as Jeremiah 31:3 tells us, "An everlasting love."

His Great Love Evokes Praise

Have you ever noticed as you sing from our hymn books how many of our beautiful hymns concern the love of God? "O Love That Wilt Not Let Me Go," "Love Lifted Me," "O Love Of God," "My Saviour's Love," and many others were written when God's wonderful love touched a heart and the Holy Spirit provoked an out-pouring of praise. Words such as "marvelous," "wonderful," "freely given," "bliss," "divine," and "boundless" fill these beautiful tributes to God whose "banner over us is love." We cannot doubt that these writers knew Him!

To express the love of God adequately would take several books. Our thoughts lead us on to chapters which might continue to express our own love and appreciation of God's love.as it blesses and regulates our lives.

But there comes a time when we must be conclusive, so we close this chapter on God's greatness with these words,

"Loved with everlasting love; Led by grace that love to know:
Spirit, breathing from above, Thou hast taught me it is so!
O, this full and perfect peace, O this transport all divine—
In a love which cannot cease, I am His and He is mine:"
(From the hymn, "I Am His and He is Mine" by Wade Robinson and James Mountain)

Questions to be considered

1. How does wisdom differ from knowledge?
2. How did Job have knowledge of the universe?
3. Explain "the fear of the Lord."
4. Name 5 ways in which the Bible describes God's greatness.
5. How is God's plan of salvation a demonstration of His greatest power?
6. What is the greatest contrast between God's works and the works of man?

CHAPTER 13

The Love of God
In Giving Us Heaven

Several years ago my family and I moved from Washington D.C. to Mansfield, Ohio. As we drove the long distance from that eastern city, we played a sort of game to relax. We would guess at what kind of house we would be moving into when we arrived in Mansfield. You see, this was near the end of World War II and houses to rent were very scarce. Because of this, we had friends in Mansfield rent us any house that was available.

We knew that we would have a house to move into but we knew very little about the house. We knew it was a large, old house and was one that author Louis Bromfield had lived in as a child. Outside of this, we knew very little about the house so we took turns guessing about what the house would look like inside and outside. We tried to see who would come close to guessing the actual truth. We were going to live in that house and we were very much interested.

One of these days, those who are redeemed by the blood of Christ are going to their heavenly home and there they are going to be forever. Therefore, we are very much interested in finding out what our heavenly home is like. So we are going to consider some facts about heaven. I am not going to give my opinion for that would be like using a candle to demonstrate the sun on a sunny day. I have never been to Heaven and do not know anything about it from personal experience. My purpose is to show you what the Word of God has to say about what heaven is like.

God has given us an infallible revelation of Himself, of His will for us, and of life after death. He has told us all that we need to know and all that is best for us to know concerning heaven. Many of the details are left out because we could never understand them, anymore than people living a 100 years ago could have understood the details of the jet age, of television, atomic power and men who walk around on the moon. But God has revealed to us the basic things that we can understand.

First of all, I want to point out the fact that heaven is a definite place, not just a fancy or a condition or a state of being.

There are people who have such a vague idea of Heaven, imagining that it is a sort of phantom world full of floating spirits. But the Heaven of the Bible is a very real place with real people, with real life; just as real and definite as these things are here on earth in our present experience.

Jesus said, "In my Father's house are many mansions (or abiding places), if it were not so I would have told you. I go and prepare a place for you and if I go and prepare a place for you I will come again and receive you unto myself that where I am there ye may be also." John 14:1-4.

When Jesus told us of our heavenly home, He said it would be a place He would prepare. Heaven is a prepared place. God has many places, many abiding places in this universe. This earth is one of them. But none of the present abiding places are good enough in the opinion of our Saviour for those for whom He died and who shall be with Him through all eternity. So He is making a new dwelling place for them.

The Lord Jesus Christ, when He arose from the grave, had a real body, a body that could eat and walk and be recognized by His disciples. He had a body that did things, as we see Him preparing breakfast for His disciples by the seashore one early morning when they had been fishing all night. The Bible says that in our resurrection bodies we shall be like the Lord Jesus. We will have real bodies, different from what they are now, but real as to their existence. These real bodies will need a real place, a real home and Heaven is a real place.

Heaven Is not only a Place but a Beautiful Place

We can be absolutely certain that anything that Jesus especially prepares for his very own will be very beautiful. There is plenty of evidence everywhere that God in His very nature has a great love for beauty and harmony. Even this earth, sin scarred and cursed as it is, bears testimony to the fact that God loves beauty. Mankind himself, who is created in God's image, has a love and an understanding of beautiful things, such as is expressed in the harmony of color in flowers, or the harmonious sounds of music, or in harmony of motion in a graceful animal. We are but creatures of God. If we then have that love for the beautiful and the harmonious, how much more so must God. AND HE IS PREPARING A PLACE FOR US.

"Eye hath not seen nor ear heard, neither have entered into the heart of man the things which God hath prepared for them that love Him." I Cor. 2:9.

This is a wonderful verse. It is the evidence that the Lord loves to make things beautiful for us.

We see it in the delicate shade of the half open rose.

We see it in the rainbow, sparkling after a shower.

We see it in the soft cheeks and twinkling eyes of little boys and girls.

We see His love for the beautiful in the colorful petticoat of the forest in October.

Just remember, the Lord who thought of these things is preparing a place for us in Heaven.

This earth has its special place of beauty and it has been my privilege to see some of them.

I have seen man-made beauty in such placed as Versailles, near Paris.

I have beheld the grandeur of the Alps in Switzerland, and stood in awe looking at the Jungfrau.

I parked my car beside the road near the base of Mt. Shasta in California and saw that mountain in the evening sunset, snow-capped and with a rosy tint gradually creeping towards its top, and I bowed my head before God in awesome wonder.

I sat at the top of the Skyline Drive and looked down into the beautiful Shenandoah Valley to behold its winding hills and the Seven Bends of the Shenandoah River.

I watched the sun set over the Golden Gate in San Francisco and stood at the base of Bridal Veil Falls in Yosemite Valley. I beheld the desert in bloom and watched the heavens bejeweled with countless stars on a cold, winter night. All of these are beautiful things on this earth. I've heard the indescribable harmonies of music, especially that harmony of human voices which thrills the soul. All of these things are wonderful. But remember, the God who has made the Grand Canyon and the desert in bloom and the bejeweled heavens is the one who is preparing a place for us. He has told us that "eye hath not seen nor ear heard, neither have entered into the heart of man the things that God hath prepared for them that love Him." Yes, Heaven is a beautiful place.

Heaven Will Be a Place of Unspoiled Joy and Happiness

The following verses contain positive statements concerning Heaven:

Psalm 16:11 "Thou wilt show me the path of life; in they presence is fullness of joy, at thy right hand there are pleasures forevermore."

Psalm 17:15 "As for me, I will behold thy face in righteousness; I shall be satisfied when I awake, with thy likeness."

Matthew 25:21 "His Lord said unto him, well done, thou good and faithful servant; thou hast been faithful over a few things, I will make thee ruler over many things; enter thou into the joy of thy Lord."

Joy! Satisfaction! Rewards! Heaven will be happiness in a new dimension.

And here are some of the things that won't be in Heaven:

Revelation 7:16, 17 "They shall hunger no more, neither thirst anymore, neither shall the sun light on them, nor any heat. For the Lamb which is in the midst of the throne shall feed them, and shall lead them unto living fountains of waters; and God shall wipe away all tears from their eyes."

Revelation 21:1, 4, 7 "And I saw a new heaven and a new earth; for the first heaven and the first earth were passed away; and there was no more sea. And God shall wipe away all tears from their eyes; and there shall be no more death, neither sorrow, nor crying, neither shall there be any more pain; for the former things are passed away. And He that sat upon the throne said, "Behold I make all things new."

Revelation 22:3-5 "And there shall be no more curse; but the throne of God and of the Lamb shall be in it; and his servants shall see his face; and his name shall be in their foreheads. And they need no candle neither light of the sun; for the Lord God giveth them light; and they shall reign forever and ever."

In heaven there will be no war and strife or hatred; peace and love will prevail.

In Heaven we will enjoy the perfect health of youth. There will be no pain or suffering. There will be no disease, no polio, no cripples, no broken bones, no cancer, no nervous breakdowns — just perfect health and no pain at all.

In heaven there will be no need for aspirins, vitamins and tranquilizers. There will be no insane asylums or other institutions for the mentally ill. In heaven there will be no hospital beds or nursing homes. There will be no caskets and sad goodbyes in a cold cemetery. In Heaven there will be no drunkenness and no lonely nights of any kind. There will be no sinful nature in Heaven, not the struggle against temptation which now is so often with us. In Heaven there will be no alarm clocks, no bills to pay, no rent to pay.

This is all a part of the beauty of heaven. But the most beautiful part of all is that we will be with Jesus!

Heaven Is a Place of Unbroken and Wonderful Fellowship

One of the interesting and yet seldom known facts about Heaven is that where the New Testament speaks about Heaven it does so in terms of fellowship, of social life, of living together, even of communities and family life.

Of course, this will not be a reproduction of life on earth, for here social life is so imperfect and often spoiled by misunderstandings and selfishness. It is broken often by marriages and death and partings and other kinds. But not so in Heaven. There living together will be perfect in fellowship.

Jesus said, "If I go and prepare a place for you, I will come again and receive you unto myself that where I am there ye may be also." John 14:3. His beloved ones are to be with Him. It speaks in Hebrews 11 of the patriarchs who looked forward to Heaven as an "abiding city." The Book of Revelation again and again speaks of a city, calling it the heavenly Jerusalem. The New Testament tells us of "the family of God in Heaven."

People are forever asking the question, "Will we recognize and know our loved ones in Heaven?" The answer to this is a very strong "yes." The Bible never argues for the existence of God. That is taken for granted. And the Bible never argues that we will know our loved ones in Heaven. That is understood, as being the normal thing. However, many passages imply that we will know our loved ones in Heaven. In I Thess. 4:13-18 Paul is comforting christian people who have loved ones who were saved and who have gone ahead of them in death. "But I would not have you to be ignorant, brethren, concerning them which are asleep, that ye sorrow not, even as others which have no hope. For if we believe that Jesus died and rose again, even so them also which sleep in Jesus will God bring with Him. For this we say unto you by the word of the Lord, that we which are alive and remain unto the coming of the Lord shall not prevent (or precede) them which are asleep. For the Lord himself shall descend from heaven with a shout, with the voice of the archangel, and with the trump of God: and the dead in Christ shall rise first. Then we which are alive and remain shall be caught up together with them in the clouds, to meet the Lord in the air; and so shall we ever be with the Lord. Wherefore comfort one another with these words." What is the comfort? That if our loved ones are saved and we are saved, we will be in a blessed reunion with one another when Jesus comes.

What comfort would there be if we would not know them, would not know if they were there? The comfort is in the fact that we will meet them, that *we will be together with them and with the Lord.*

Heaven is a place of fellowship. There will be no reproductions of earthly relationships and social life, but there will be the heavenly counterpart of those things.

Heaven Is now Waiting for Man to Enter

Yes, Heaven is open and waiting for the fellowship of man. Mankind is wanted up there. This is one of the great stories of the Bible.

Paul says in Philippians 3:20, "Our citizenship is in heaven." In II Cor. 5:1 we read, "For we know that if our earthly house of this tabernacle were dissolved, we have a building of God, a house not made with hands, eternal in the heavens."

Jesus said to His disciples who were beside themselves with joy in being able to perform miracles in His Name, according to Luke 10:20, "Notwithstanding in this rejoice not, that the spirits are subject unto you; but rather rejoice because your names are written in Heaven."

When I was a boy in Europe I dreamed about America. I read every line that told about this country that I could find. I wanted to go there with all my heart. Finally, when I was 21 years old I went through a rigid process of securing an immigration visa which would allow me to come to this land and become a citizen here. After some time, I secured that precious piece of paper and as soon as I could arrange passage I came here to the land of my dreams. While I was successful in getting here, many who wanted to come here were turned down. Immigration to this land is restricted, very restricted indeed. There are people today by the millions who long to come to America but who cannot leave their own land and who cannot secure entrance here. What good does it do for them to read about the freedom of this land when they are not permitted to enter?

But not so in Heaven! There man is wanted. There is even rejoicing in Heaven over one who decides to come. This is the great wisdom in the great, wide sea.

According to the record in Genesis, God "made" the sun, moon and stars on the fourth day. It is of importance that we take special notice of the word "made" which in the Hebrew is the word "Asah." It stands in contrast to the Hebrew word "Borah" which is translated "created." The word "created" is used in three different verses in the first chapter of Genesis. We find it in verses 1, 21 and 27. To create means to bring into existence something out of nothing by the simple use of power. It is used each time where we are told that God brought into existence something new which had not existed in any form, namely, the creation of the universe, (Genesis 1:10), the creation of life, (Genesis 1:21), and the creation of man with spiritual life (Genesis 1:27).

The word "Asah" translated "made" in Gen. one, means to arrange, to organize into the desired form, as for example when man takes wool and organizes or makes it into a fine suit. We understand that the sun, moon and stars were already created in the original creation, but on the fourth day God arranged or organized them into the desired system to perform His purpose regarding the earth. The purpose of these heavenly bodies is to give light, heat, day and night, and the seasons and the years. The heavens display the glory of God and also His great wisdom.

The first foreign immigrant to this earth was the Son of God from Heaven who came down to open His own country to us. The Bible is His inspired circular, printed in many languages, inviting men to come to Heaven.

As I think of this, there are three things that amaze me.

1. I am amazed at the condition or terms of entrance into Heaven. Just what are the requirements for entering Heaven?

In Revelation 21:27 we read, "And there shall in no wise enter into it anything that defileth, neither whatsoever worketh abomination, or maketh a lie, but they which are written in the Lamb's Book of Life." Also read I Cor. 6:9, 10. The Word of God certainly teaches that Heaven is a perfect place where only righteousness can dwell. Any type of sin or disobedience cannot be allowed to enter. We could not expect it to be otherwise.

The perfect Son of God came from Heaven to make full atonement for the sin of man. He died to pay the penalty so that we might receive salvation and righteousness as a gift from God. Since Heaven is a perfect place He made it possible that we might be made perfect in the Son. "For he hath made him to be sin for us, who knew no sin; that we might be made the righteousness of God in him (II Cor. 5:21). There is no way that we can pay for our heavenly passport. It is completely free, not of our works for "By grace are ye saved through faith" (Eph. 2:8-10).

Heaven is open to all people who will recognize their need as sinners and come to God by way of the Christ of the cross, for there and there alone can God forgive and receive sinful man. This is the Gospel, the good news of God to man.

2. I am amazed that so few people seem to be concerned about going to heaven.

As we consider how wonderful and beautiful Heaven really is, and as we consider the unbelievable sacrifice that God has made to provide a free entrance for every person who will come by faith in Christ, you would think that all men and women would make sure of getting there. But just the opposite is true. The great majority of people who know about Heaven pay no real attention to it. Jesus wept over this terrible indifference of man: "O Jerusalem, Jerusalem, thou that killest the prophets and stonest them which are sent unto thee, how often would I have gathered thy children together even as a hen gathereth her chickens under her wings, and ye would not." Matt. 23:37. Also read Matt. 7:13, 14 and John 3:19.

There are two factors that enter here. One is man's lack of humility and his abundance of human pride. If we could sell salvation and heaven at high prices, people would stand in line to buy it. But when it is offered as a free gift, we ignore it.

To you Christian friends who are looking forward to Heaven, let me plead with you to put first things first in life now. Let us live such lives as will show the Lord our appreciation for His wonderful salvation. Let us invest our lives in those things which count toward that Heavenly life, both for ourselves and others.

"I believe that someday,
Through His boundless love and saving grace,
I shall rise on wings of light to realms above,
I'll see His face.
There beyond the earth and air and sea and sky,
I'll dwell with Him, no more to die,
O this, praise God, I believe."

Questions For Discussion

1. What will be different in our bodies in heaven?
2. What will be different in our environment?
3. What will be the "greatest joy" of heaven?

4. From what will we be delivered?

Suggested Reading
The Love of God in Giving Us Heaven

Jesus feeding the disciples by the sea	John 21:1-4
On the road to Emmaus	Luke 24:13-33
Appearance to the disciples	Luke 24:36-44
The Ascension into the clouds	Matt. 28:17-20

BIBLIOGRAPHY

Barnhouse, Donald Grey, *Words Fitly Spoken*, Tyndale House Publishers.

Charnock, Stephen, *The Existence and Attributes of God*, Kregel Publications.

Halverson, Richard C., *The Gospel for the Whole of Life*, Zondervan Publishing House.

Lang, G. H., *The Parabolic Teaching of Scripture*, Wm. B. Eerdmans Publishing Company.

Morgan, G. Campbell D. D., *The Parables and Metaphors of Our Lord*, Fleming H. Revell Co.

Rice, Edwin W. D. D., *People's Commentary on the Gospel According to Mark*, The American Sunday-School Union.

Sanders, Oswald J., *Christ Incomparable*, Christian Literature Crusade.

Sanders, Oswald J., *The Incomparable Christ*, Moody Press.

Sauer, Erich, *The Triumph of the Crucified*, Wm. B. Eerdmans Publishing Company.

Warfield, Benjamin Breckinridge, The Person and Work of Christ, The Presbyterian and Reformed Publishing Company.

ADDITIONAL STUDY GUIDES IN THIS SERIES . . .

GENESIS, John P. Burke
EXODUS, Tom Julien
DEUTERONOMY, Bernard N. Schneider
JOSHUA, JUDGES & RUTH, John J. Davis
1 & 2 SAMUEL & 1 KINGS 1-11, John J. Davis
KINGS & CHRONICLES, John C. Whitcomb
JOB THROUGH SONG OF SOLOMON, Gerald H. Twombly
PROVERBS, Charles W. Turner
DANIEL, Robert D. Culver
THE MINOR PROPHETS, Gerald H. Twombly
MATTHEW, Harold H. Etling
MARK, Homer A. Kent, Jr.
GOSPEL OF JOHN, Homer A. Kent, Jr.
ACTS, Homer A. Kent, Jr.
ROMANS, Herman A. Hoyt
1 CORINTHIANS, James L. Boyer
2 CORINTHIANS, Homer A. Kent, Jr.
GALATIANS, Homer A. Kent, Jr.
EPHESIANS, Tom Julien
PHILIPPIANS, David L. Hocking
COLOSSIANS AND PHILEMON, Homer A. Kent, Jr.
1 & 2 TIMOTHY, Dean Fetterhoff
HEBREWS, Herman A. Hoyt
JAMES, Roy R. Roberts
2 PETER, Herman A. Hoyt
1, 2, 3 JOHN, Raymond E. Gingrich
REVELATION, Herman A. Hoyt
THE WORLD OF UNSEEN SPIRITS, Bernard N. Schneider
THE HOLY SPIRIT AND YOU, Bernard N. Schneider
PROPHECY, THINGS TO COME, James L. Boyer
PULPIT WORDS TRANSLATED FOR PEW PEOPLE, Charles W. Turner
SWEETER THAN HONEY, Jesse B. Deloe *(A guide to effective Bible study and the background of how we got our Bible)*
BRETHREN BELIEFS AND PRACTICES, Harold H. Etling
THE FAMILY FIRST, Kenneth O. Gangel
LESSONS IN LEADERSHIP FROM THE BIBLE, Kenneth O. Gangel

Obtain from your local Christian bookstore or request an order blank from BMH Books, P. O. Box 544, Winona Lake, IN 46590